Advancing Secure Image Handling

Through Chaotic and Bio-Molecular Computing

Advancing Secure Image Handling
Through Chaotic and Bio-Molecular Computing

Exploring the Role of Chaotic and Bio-Molecular Computing in Image Security

Sujarani Rajendran
Manivannan Doraipandian

EXCELLER BOOKS®
A GLOBAL PRESS

Advancing Secure Image Handling through Chaotic and Bio-Molecular Computing

Exploring the Role of Chaotic and Bio-Molecular Computing in Image Security

Cover by Exceller Books using resources from Pixabay.com

ISBN: 978-93-48892-21-8

First published in India in 2025 by Exceller Books,
An imprint of GE Group

Address: G1, Dream Apartment, Degree College Road, Belgharia,
Kolkata, 700056, India
www.excellerbooks.com

EXCELLER BOOKS®
A GLOBAL PRESS

Dedications

The Almighty

&

My Beloved Father

Acknowledgements

With the blessings of Almighty, this research work was carried out and has come to a logical end. I wish to express my sincere thanks to all those who helped me during the course of this journey and also backed me in my research career.

Firstly, I would like to thank my research advisor Dr. D. Manivannan, Associate Professor (CSE), School of Computing. I am thankful to him for the freedom he has given, which enabled me to think and work independently.

My sincere thanks to Prof. R. Sethuraman, Chancellor and Dr. S. Vaidhyasubramaniam,

Vice-Chancellor of SASTRA Deemed University, for providing me an opportunity to carry out my doctoral studies in this esteemed University.

I express my sincere thanks to Dr. S. Swaminathan, Director, Center for Nanotechnology & Advanced Biomaterials (CeNTAB) and Dean (Planning and Development) for his guidance in all aspects during this period of research.

I would like to extend my sincere thanks to Dr. R. Chandramouli (Registrar), Dr. S. Jayalalitha (Dean Research), and Dr. B. Santhi (Associate Dean – Research, SoC) for their constant support and encouragement.

I wish to express my sincere thanks to Dr. A. Umamakeswari (Dean, SoC), and Dr. V. Ramaswamy (Dean, SRC), for their constant support and encouragement in all aspects of my research work.

I wish to acknowledge my doctoral committee members, Dr. K. Kannan (Dean, School of Education), Dr. C. Mala, Professor, NIT, Trichy, Dr. N.P. Gopalan, Professor, NIT, Trichy and Dr. K.S. Ravichandran for their critical comments and suggestions.

I wish to express my most sincere gratitude to my mentor Dr. K. Kannan (Dean, School of Education), for his tireless encouragement, support and patience during my Ph.D. candidature. He is truly a great inspiration for me.

I would like to express my sincere and special thanks to Dr. R. John Bosco Balagruru,

Dean (Sponsored Research), School of Electrical & Electronics Engineering (SEEE) and Center for Nanotechnology & Advanced Biomaterials (CeNTAB), for his support to carry out my work.

My special thanks to Dr. V. Padma Priya (Senior Assistant Professor, SEEE), Dr. Chanthini Baskar and Dr. Dhivya Ravichandran for their encouragement, suggestions and support to carry out this work.

I also thank Mrs. S. Ramya (Assistant Professor, SoC), Mr. S. Ananthakrishnan (Assistant Professor, SoC), Mr. S. Palanivel (Assistant Professor, (SoC), who were very supportive to carry out my work.

All these years of perseverance and achievement will be incomplete without my mother Mrs. R. Suseela. Sincere gratitude to my mother in law Mrs. K. Rajathi, a strong pillar of support and my life partner Mr. K. Ramesh, who was the great motivation behind my education. My uncle Mr. S. Kodilingam, who backed me with his moral support and helped me to achieve heightsin my education.

I take this opportunity to thank all the people helped me throughout this journey of my life.

Thanks to all
Sujarani Rajendran

Table of Contents

List of Tables 9
List of Figures 11
Overview 15

CHAPTER 1
Introduction 17
CHAPTER 2
Non-Linear Chaos-Based Image Cryptosystems: A Review 41
CHAPTER 3
Pseudo-Random Number Generation Based on Fusional Chaotic Maps 72
CHAPTER 4
A Novel Cross Cosine Map Based Medical Image Cryptosystem Using Dynamic Bit-Level Diffusion 85
CHAPTER 5
Fast Pre-processing Hex Chaos Triggered Color Image Cryptosystem 117
CHAPTER 6
Lightweight Bio-crypt Architecture to Secure Biometric Templates on IoT Applications 147
CHAPTER 7
Conclusion 178

Appendix A: List of Publications 173

List of Tables

Table 2.1: Relationships and variations between chaos theory and cryptology

Table 2.2: Summarization of the governing equations, parameter range, randomness and merits of 1D chaotic maps

Table 2.3: Summarization of the governing equations and parameter range of 2D chaotic map

Table 2.4: Summarization of the governing equations and parameter range of 2D chaotic map

Table 3.1: NIST test suite results of 2D CCM

Table 4.1: Comparison of CC results with existing state of the art

Table 4.2: Results of Global and Local Shannon Entropy of different test images

Table 4.3: Key Sensitivity Analysis

Table 4.4: Results and comparison of NPCR and UACI metrics

Table 4.5: Parameters of encryption and decryption Quality

Table 4.6: Comparison of performance metrics regarding statistical and differential attacks

Table 5.1: Comparison of key series generation: Number of Preprocessing (No. of. PP), Processing Time (PT) and memory between proposed and existing systems

Table 5.2: Results of correlation coefficient and Shannon entropy analysis for SIPI color image database

Table 5.3: Comparison of the average correlation coefficients and global Shannon entropy of Lena image

Table 5.4: NPCR and UACI values of different test images with keys K1 and K2

Table 5.5: Comparison of key sensitivity with one bit difference of Lena (4.2.04)

Table 5.6: Results of EQ, PSNR and SSIM for different test images
Table 5.7: Comparison of PSNR and EQ with existing systems
Table 5.8: Estimation of decryption quality based on SSIM results
Table 5.9: Comparison of color image encryption
Table 5.10: Comparison of greyscale image encryption
Table 6.1: DNA encoding rules
Table 6.2: DNA addition table
Table 6.3: DNA XOR table
Table 6.4: DNA encoding mapping table for Rule 2
Table 6.5: Comparison of DNA Encoding, DNA Encryption for 256 x 256 image
Table 6.6: Comparison of correlation coefficient and entropy result of Fingerprint template
Table 6.7: Comparison of Entropy and correlation result of Palmprint template
Table 6.8: Decryption quality against transmission attacks using 003_l_460_02

List of Figures

Figure 1.1: Comparison of data breaches and exposure between 2018 and 2019 (Source: https://www.idtheftcenter.org/wp-content/uploads/2020/01/01.28.2020_ITRC_2019-End-of-Year-Data-Breach-Report)

Figure 1.2: Major components of information security

Figure 1.3: Safeguarding images during transmission and storage

Figure1.4: Diagrammatical representation of the overall research work

Figure 1.5: General architecture of chaos and DNA based image cryptosystems

Figure 2.1: Basic inherent properties of chaotic systems

Figure 2.2: Architecture of image encryption

Figure 2.3: Different types of One Dimensional Chaotic map

Figure 2.4: Transposition using 1D logistic map

Figure 2.5: Different types of 2D chaotic map

Figure 2.6: Image Confusion (a) Original image (b) Result of first iteration of confusion (c) Output of second iteration (d) Output of second iteration (e) Final confused image after tenth iteration

Figure 2.7: Chaos attractors of Lorenz map (a) X-Y plane (b) Y-Z plane (c) X-Z plane

Figure 2.8: Histogram of (a) Original image (b) Cipher image

Figure 3.1: Spatiotemporal diagram of 2D CCM system a) X series b) Y series

Figure 3.2: Chaotic behaviour analysis of 2D CCM a) Lyapunov exponent b) Bifurcation diagram c) Trajectories of X and Y

Figure 4.1: Architecture of 2D CCM based medical image cryptosystem

Figure 4.2: Illustration of the confusion process a) i, IX series denote the row of the image b) j, IY series denote the columns of the Image c) Illustration of row permutation with 10 Pixels d) Original image and their corresponding confused image

Figure 4.3: Demonstration of Bits-Flipping using a single 8-bit pixel value for all possible flip bits

Figure 4.4: Sample medical images: (a-h) 256 x 256 (8-bit image), (i-l) 512 x 512 (16-bit image)

Figure 4.5: Histogram Analysis: (a, b and c) Original image and its histogram (d, e and f) Corresponding cipher image and its histogram

Figure 4.6: Key sensitivity analysis: Plot of three encrypted images using key1, key2 and key3

Figure 4.7: Crop attack analysis: Cipher image with (a) 0.5% Data Loss (b) 1.0% Data Loss (c) 2.0% Data Loss (d) 5.0% Data Loss (e, f, g and h) Decrypted images of corresponding cropped cipher image (a, b, c and d)

Figure 4.8: Graphical representation for the comparison results a) CC b) NPCR, UACI and Entropy c) CC of image size 512 x 512

Figure 5.1: Chaotic attractor of Lorenz hyper chaotic map a) X_Y phase b) Y_Z phase c) Z_W phase

Figure 5.2: Generation of integer chaotic series using hexadecimal conversion and fragmentation

Figure 5.3: Randomness of integer format chaotic series: chaotic attractor of IX series

Figure 5.4: Block view of the proposed image cryptosystem

Figure 5.5: Demonstration of merging and circular shift operation

Figure 5.6: Experimental outcome: Original image and their corresponding confused and diffused image

Figure 5.7: Histogram analysis between RGB components of original and ciphered pepper image

Figure 5.8: Correlation coefficient analysis: Correlation of pixels in (b and f) horizontal direction of Red component (c and g) vertical direction of Green component (d and h) diagonal direction of Blue component

Figure 5.9: Key sensitivity analysis (a) Original image (b) Ciphered image with original keys (c) Ciphered image with changed keys (d) Difference between (c) and (d)

Figure 5.10: Analysis of cropping attack: Encrypted Lena cropped by the ratio of (a) 1/16 (b) 1/8 (c) 1/4 (d) 1/2. (e-h) Corresponding decrypted images of (a-d)

Figure 5.11: Noise attack analysis (a) Decrypted image not affected by noise (b, c and d) Decrypted cipher images affected by salt and pepper noise of intensities 0.01, 0.1 and 0.2; (e, f, g and h) Decrypted cipher images

Figure 6.1: Framework of IoT environment in various applications

Figure 6.2: Demonstration of proposed DNA encoding and DNA encryption

Figure 6.3: Outline of the biomolecular and chaos based biometric cryptosystem

Figure 6.4: Result of confusion phase (a) Original image (b, c) ODD and EVEN image (d, e) Confused ODD and EVEN image (f) Final confused image

Figure 6.5: Experimental result: (a) Original image (b) Confused image (c) Diffused image (d) Decrypted image

Figure 6.6: Experimental Results: First row shows the original fingerprint images. Second row shows its corresponding cipher images

Figure 6.7: Histogram Analysis: (a) Original fingerprint histogram

Figure 6.8: Correlation Analysis. Original and cipher image pixel correlation between pixels among (a) Horizontal Direction (HD) (b) Vertical Direction (VD) (c) Diagonal Direction (DD)

Figure 6.9: Key sensitivity analysis: Plot of cipher image encrypted by two different keys key1 and key2

Figure 6.10: Robustness analysis against crop attack: (first row) cipher image cropped by specific range (a) (50 x 50) (b) (75 x 75) (c) (125 x 125). (second row) Corresponding decrypted image. (third row) Decrypted image after applied the median filter

Figure 6.11: Noise attack analysis: Decrypted image after applied the median filter: salt and pepper noise with range (a) 0.001 (b) 0.01 (c) 0.1

Overview

Rapid development in digital technology has led to sensitive information communication over public and private networks. In this scenario, the security and confidentiality of sensitive information transmitted by key applications have become a matter of great concern. On the one hand, technology has made information freely accessible to all, but on the other, it has critically endangered the security of data transmitted via networks. Among the various types of digital data, images carry great significance in many key areas like banking, biometric authentication, and social media. Hence, there is a pressing need to secure sensitive images while transmitted via insecure networks. Cryptography plays a vital role in protecting the confidentiality of sensitive images. In recent times, chaos and DNA based cryptography have emerged as a promising solution to secure images due to their desirable properties. The present study combines DNA and chaos in a single system and attempts to develop a novel DNA and chaos crypt architecture for securing images. Compared to traditional cryptosystems, the proposed method offers optimal security to images and is highly suitable for image security algorithms. The present study aims to design, develop and analyse the performance of new chaos and DNA based image cryptosystem. Initially, a fusional Cross Cosine Map (CCM) is developed to generate the required chaotic key series for the image cryptosystem. The proposed image cryptosystem uses a chaotic key series generated by the CCM to perform confusion and diffusion processes on greyscale medical images to secure their confidentiality. Additionally, a hyper chaos based image cryptosystem is developed to enhance the confidentiality of color images using a hexadecimal pre-processing technique. Finally, integrated and lightweight crypt architecture is designed using chaos and DNA cryptography to achieve double-layered security of biometric images.

In order to assess the effectiveness and strength of the developed cryptosystems, statistical, differential, robustness attack analyses and key size, key sensitivity, and computational complexity analyses are performed extensively. Standard statistical measures like Mean Square Error (MSE), Peak Signal to Noise Ratio (PSNR), Encryption Quality (EQ), and Structural Similarity Index Measure (SSIM) are quantified to evaluate the encryption and decryption quality of images.

CHAPTER 1
Introduction

1.1. Motivation

The domain of digital technology has witnessed phenomenal growth in recent decades, leading to a manifold increase in the use of images in different applications like e-banking, e-learning, e-healthcare, and e-military communications. In the domain of e-healthcare, medical images are widely used to store sensitive medical data of patients and diagnose diseases. In e-banking and e-military applications, digital images act as an authentication attribute to access sensitive data. On popular social media websites, sensitive color images of individuals are stored and transmitted. With such extensive use of images in key application areas, the need to protect these images during storage and transmission has become essential to avoid data breaches.

According to the Identity Theft Resource Center (ITRC) 2019 year-end report [1], 1,473 data breaches were reported in 2019, which is 17% higher than the breaches reported in 2018 (1,257 breaches). As reported by International Business Machines (IBM) Corporation in 2019, the cost of a data breach has increased by 12% over the past five years across all industries, and now the cost has reached $3.92 million on average [2]. Data breaches result in reduced consumer trust, loss of reputation, and severe financial loss. There is a growing concern to ensure data confidentiality, authenticity, and integrity in order to prevent fraud and forgery during the transmission and storage of sensitive images. This can be achieved through encryption, key management, and hashing techniques.

Conventional algorithms like Advanced Encryption Standard (AES), Data Encryption Standard (DES), and International Data Encryption Algorithm (IDEA) have been applied for securing images. Owing to the inherent qualities of images, such as large data size, a higher repetition rate of pixels, and higher correlation among picture elements, conventional algorithms fail to provide optimal security. Additionally, they require high computational time, power consumption, and memory [3][4]. To address these limitations, newly developed security algorithms have adopted chaotic systems to increase throughput at a comparatively lower cost. Chaotic systems have specific inbuilt features such as randomness, deterministic and ergodic properties, and higher sensitivity to initial conditions. These desirable features help enhance the security of images at lower costs [5]. Since chaotic systems are widely employed for developing image cryptosystems, the developed chaotic crypto model can effectively provide security for images during transmission and storage over insecure networks.

1.2. Need for Information Security

In the present scenario, cybercrimes are carried out with the intent of breaching data security and exposing sensitive records of individuals and businesses. Key sectors like business, education, healthcare, military, and finance are usually the targets of such cybercrime exploits. According to the ITRC report shown in Figure 1.1, many industries were seriously affected by data breaches and exposure. Predominantly in 2019, the exposure of sensitive records increased in the healthcare, banking, and education sectors compared to 2018. Additionally, the healthcare data breach cost reached $429 per record, the highest of any industry for the ninth straight year [6]. The number of data breaches across all industries also increased in 2019 compared to 2018.

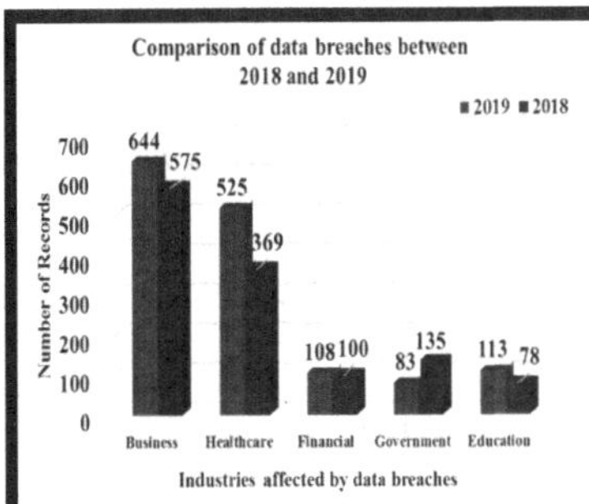

Comparison of sensitive records exposure between 2018 and 2019

INDUSTRY	NUMBER OF SENSITIVE RECORDS EXPOSED -2019	NUMBER OF SENSITIVE RECORDS EXPOSED -2018
Business	18,824,975	438,952,056
Healthcare	39,378,157	10,632,600
Banking/Financial	100,621,770	18,447,92
Government	3,606,114	17,78,658
Education	2,252,439	1,414,624
Total Reports	164,683,455	471,225,862

Figure 1.1: Comparison of Data Breaches and Exposure between 2018 and 2019 (Source: https://www.idtheftcenter.org/wp-content/uploads/2020/01/01.28.2020_ITRC_2019-End-of-Year-Data-Breach-Report)

According to an IBM report, data breaches in India cost about Rs 14 crore on average between August 2019 and April 2020 [7], and the largest data breach in India is the government's ID database, Aadhaar, which includes individuals' sensitive facial and biometric images. It reportedly suffered multiple breaches that potentially compromised the records of all 1.1 billion registered citizens [8]. In parallel to this ID data breach, Antheous Tecnologia, a biometric solution firm, exposed over 81.5 million employee records, which included emails, phone numbers, and unique fingerprints of employees [9].

The two core factors that increased the breaches and exposure in various e-applications are:

1. Identity theft aims to collect the sensitive identity information of a user and use it for impersonation.

2. Absence of adequate protection and mindfulness against security assaults in e-application services.

Careless administration of valuable electronic data may result in the massive failure of the entire e-application services framework. It might entice hackers to force entry, steal, modify, and erase sensitive private data. The exposure of private data leads to mass panic, customer dissatisfaction and loss, severe financial losses, and other extreme consequences, such as the sudden closure of large businesses.

Cyberattacks on IoT devices endanger the privacy, security, and valuable data of individuals and commercial entities. They threaten the very development and existence of the IoT field and have made security a keyword in the IoT environment. Hewlett Packard reports that 70% of common IoT devices are vulnerable to various types of attacks [10]. IoT devices have many inherent flaws owing to the absence of encrypted transmission, incompetent authentication and authorization, poor security configuration, and lack of physical security.

According to the survey, the most affected multimedia content in data breaches is digital images due to unauthorized access/disclosure. As a result, this research focuses on protecting digital images from unauthorized access/disclosure during transmission and storage.

1.3. Major Components of Security Services

Fundamental security components for establishing a secure framework are as follows:

(a) Confidentiality (C) - Ensuring electronic information is accessed only by authorized individuals.

(b) Integrity (I) - Ensuring digital data is reliable and has not been subtly modified or altered by any unauthorized person.
(c) Authentication (A) - Guaranteeing the source of data and ensuring information belongs to the correct entity—identifying the real users in two-party communication.
The main components of the secure framework are illustrated in Figure 1.2. These three major components of information security services are stated as "C-I-A".

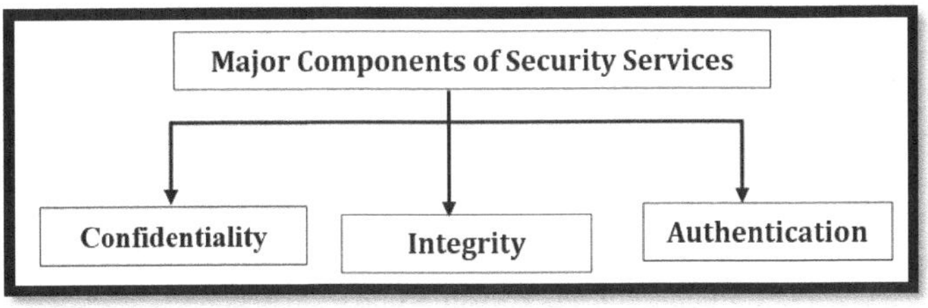

Figure 1.2. : Major Components of Information Security

1.4. Current Solutions for Safeguarding Digital Images

In the domain of high-end web innovation, the most prominent and driving constraint related to the transmission of multimedia information, including text, images, audio, and video, is data security. Compared to the transmission of audio and video data, the rate of image transmission is high. Hence, image security has become a key concern in multiple applications such as e-healthcare, e-banking, e-learning, and personal and military communications. One of the best solutions for safeguarding multimedia content from breaches is maintaining C-I-A during storage and transmission phases, as shown in Figure 1.3.

As illustrated in Figure 1.3, the three key security components of C-I-A can be achieved by applying encryption, hashing, and key management. Hence, cryptography proves to be an appropriate field for protecting multimedia content, especially images, during storage and transmission.

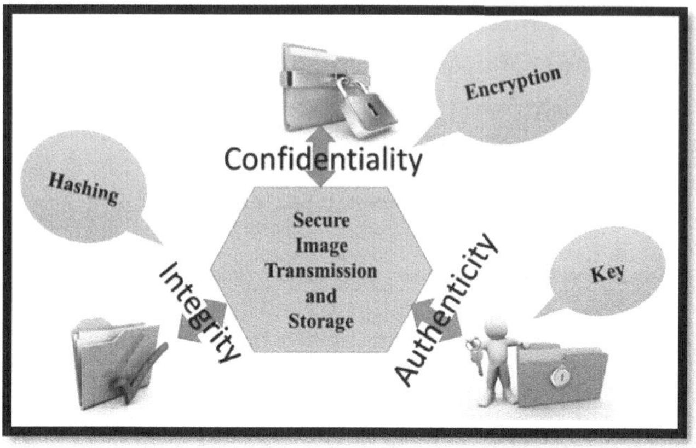

*Figure **Error! No text of specified style in document.**.1 : Safeguarding Images during Transmission and Storage*

1.5. Image Encryption

The main idea behind encryption is to transmit an image securely through a network so that an unauthenticated client cannot decrypt the image and view it. Different researchers have proposed various image cryptosystems for securing images by adopting different techniques like symmetric, asymmetric, compressive, and selective encryption. These encryption methodologies are discussed in the following subsections. In connection with this, in this thesis, efficient image cryptosystems have been developed by combining chaos and DNA computing for secure image transmission and storage.

1.5.1. Conventional Symmetric Key Image Encryption Techniques

AES is a famous symmetric encryption algorithm proposed in 1999 by Rijmen and Daemen [11]. The primary purpose of developing this algorithm was to encrypt textual content. Later, various researchers adapted this algorithm for image encryption with a few changes in functionalities to improve its efficiency. The AES algorithm has its own drawbacks when adapted for image encryption, such as high computational cost, processing power, memory, and bandwidth requirements.

In order to overcome this problem, Zainal et al. [12] enhanced the efficiency of AES by applying three modifications. Firstly, the ten rounds of the mix column process were reduced to five rounds to lessen encryption delay. Secondly, the security of the algorithm was enhanced by adding the mix column operation in the key schedule process. Lastly, to decrease the complexity of hardware configuration, the S-box and Inverse S-box were replaced with a single S-box to be used for both ciphering and deciphering. The modified AES algorithm has better security and efficiency than the original AES.

Riaz et al. [13] proposed a new modified AES algorithm by interchanging the mix column step with permutation, as the mix column step increases execution time. Additionally, the number of rounds was changed based on input size to make the algorithm more efficient for any size of data. Different researchers have modified the original AES at different times to make the algorithm more suitable for image encryption.

Upadhyay et al. [14] presented a symmetric image encryption technique based on IDEA. They converted the 24-bit pixels into a 64-bit representation and applied the IDEA algorithm over each 64-bit pixel to obtain the cipher image. A new color image encryption method was developed by Manishkumar et al. [15] by utilizing the generalized Vigenère-type table. Similarly, different researchers have developed various symmetric key-based image cryptosystems to achieve optimal image encryption [16].

1.5.2. Asymmetric Key Image Encryption Techniques

Many applications do not have a safe channel to transfer the private key or the means to keep the decryption key private, so public key cryptography has to be relied upon. Public key cryptography is a straightforward method for creating an imparted secret key over a validated communication channel without using a previously imparted secret key. The majority of traditional public key cryptosystems are designed to encrypt text data. However, a few works on public key image encryption have been developed.

Guleria et al. [17] fabricated a new encryption technique for color images by applying the Rivest, Shamir, Adleman (RSA) cryptosystem on each channel of the color image and executing Discrete Cosine Transform (DCT) on each encrypted channel to transform the spatial value channels into frequency channels. Finally, the processed channels were dislocated using the Arnold transform to obtain encrypted channels.

A new asymmetric image cryptosystem [18] was proposed by combining the Elliptic Curve with the Hill cipher, where a rectilinear multiplication matrix was used to generate keys that can withstand exhaustive attacks. Mingguanh Shan et al. [19] proposed an asymmetric image cipher using a phase-truncated Fractional Fourier Transform (FFT). Further, pixel confusion and a random phase mask were applied to make the image completely noisy. The same authors developed another asymmetric cryptosystem using DCT instead of FFT [20].

First, the DCT of each image was cropped using a low-pass filter and converted into a spectrum signal equal to the size of the image. Then, the signals were transformed into spatial values. The encrypted image was constructed using a conditional decomposition function.

An image cryptosystem was formulated using Elliptic Curve Cryptography (ECC) by Ismail et al. [21]. In that cryptosystem, elliptic curve point addition was used for key generation as the first stage of encryption. In the second stage, an XOR operation was executed between the partially encrypted images using a pseudo key sequence generated by sine, cosine, and tent maps. After two stages of encryption, the encrypted image was digitally signed to maintain integrity and authenticity.

Numerous researchers have developed different asymmetric image cryptosystems using ECC, RSA, DCT, and FFT, achieving optimal security in key sharing compared to symmetric cryptosystems.

1.5.3. Image Compression and Encryption

Different image cryptosystems have been developed to achieve secure storage and transmission of images. However, when the image transmission rate increases, the available bandwidth places strain on real-time applications. In order to overcome this issue, compression techniques have been adapted in the field of image encryption, and many Compressive Sensing (CS)-based image cryptosystems have been proposed.

Li et al. [22] proposed a secure digital image cryptosystem using CS and dual random phase encoding. First, the original image was compressed using CS, and its values were quantized using a sigmoid map. Then, the cipher image was generated using confusion and substitution. In between these processes, authentication data was embedded in the values generated by CS.

A digital image compression and encryption methodology based on CS and cyclic shift was proposed in [23]. A Gauss matrix and sparse Fourier transform were used to compress images, and a cyclic shift was executed for permutation. The algorithm works in three stages: Chebyshev map is used to generate the key and reduce complexity in key transmission, the Sigmoid function in CS is used to reduce the image transmission rate and make the algorithm applicable for real-time image encryption and transmission.

Wardoyo et al. [24] developed a model of compression and encryption with dynamic and symmetric key generation and distribution. The generated key was encrypted twice using the RSA algorithm to ensure authenticity and confidentiality. The encrypted key was updated in the encrypted image and placed at the end of the file.

Kehui et al. [25] proposed an image cryptosystem that combines CS and hyper-chaotic function. This cryptosystem is a combination of confusion, compression, and substitution processes. First, the original image is transformed using Discrete Wavelet Transform (DWT), and a concerned matrix is obtained. Then, permutation is executed on each row and column using a key sequence generated by a two-dimensional infinite modulation map. Finally, Galois field multiplication is applied to the cipher image in the diffusion phase. Different compression and encryption-based image cryptosystems have been developed [26], [27].

1.5.4. Selective Image Encryption

Effective compression-based encryption systems achieved good encryption results. However, many of the algorithms suffered from computational overhead and limited compression capabilities. Partially encrypted multimedia communication was seen as a feasible solution for low-power, lesser memory-consuming, high-speed, and real-time security. Recently, different partial encryption methodologies have been developed by many researchers.

Murali et al. [28] proposed a selective image cryptosystem using square wave confusion of orthogonal polynomial values. Both confusion and diffusion were executed on the Region of Interest (RoI), while the other portions of the image were confused by applying square-wave shuffling. The developed algorithm can be employed in both the frequency and spatial domains. It is also compatible with the Android operating system.

Hore et al. [29] proposed another selective encryption method based on dactylology-based feature extraction. The algorithm has two phases— in the first phase, a gesture key is used to identify RoI, and in the second phase, the generated session key is used for encryption. The new scheme improves security without compromising the quality of the image.

Despite various researchers proposing different image encryption techniques for protecting digital images, each technique has flaws in terms of security or performance. These flaws are addressed in the following section.

1.6. Limit Ations of Existing Image Cryptosystems

Conventional algorithms like symmetric AES, DES, and IDEA, and asymmetric RSA and ECC [33] have been applied for securing images. Owing to the inherent qualities of images, such as large data size, high repetition rate of pixels, and strong correlation among picture elements, traditional algorithms fail to provide optimal security [34].

Data compression has long been recognized as a valuable cryptographic method. An ideal data compression algorithm can convert a redundant message into a non-repetitive source. As a result, recent image cryptosystem research has focused on combining image compression with encryption to reduce the execution time of both encoding and decoding during image transmission, storage, and processing. However, these techniques require additional execution time and memory, and in some situations, they create encryption-related problems in compressed data [35]. Some researchers performed encryption before compression, but this reduced the efficiency of compression.

To overcome this drawback, selective image encryption was proposed, wherein only the sensitive part of the image is encrypted instead of encrypting the entire image. The main objective of this technique is to minimize the portion of the image that needs to be encrypted while maintaining an optimal trade-off between computational complexity and execution time, still achieving security with minimal time in real-time communication systems. However, one of the most significant issues encountered in this technique is the manual selection of the encryption region [36].

Therefore, a robust encryption methodology is required to overcome these issues and achieve optimal encryption at a low computational cost and complexity. Different researchers have identified chaos-based cryptosystems as an efficient approach for securing images. Numerous chaos-based image encryption algorithms have been proposed by various researchers. Even though chaotic cryptographic architectures provide efficient security, Farah et al. [37] have confirmed that a chaotic system alone is insufficient to provide a high level of security for sensitive images.

To address this issue, this research work focuses on combining chaos and biomolecular DNA cryptography schemes to accomplish a dual-layer, efficient image encryption mechanism that fulfills the complete security requirements for secure image transmission and storage on unsecured channels. The overall research focus is illustrated in Figure 1.4.

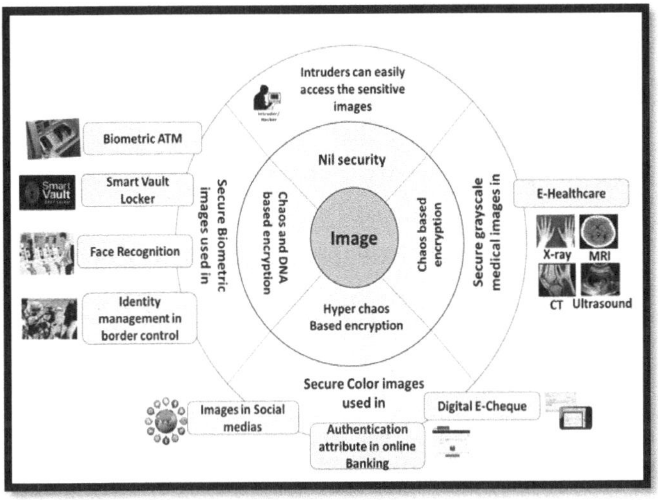

Figure 1.4: Diagrammatical Representation of the Overall Research Work

1.7. Need for Chaos and DNA-Based Image Cryptosystem

To overcome the limitations of traditional encryption techniques, various methodologies for image encryption have been developed. Among them, chaos-based image encryption is considered highly adaptable and suitable for all types and sizes of images. It fascinates researchers due to its randomness, determinism, ergodicity, and high sensitivity to initial parameters [38]. These desirable features make chaos-based image cryptosystems a suitable choice for image encryption.

The following are the merits of chaos-based cryptosystems over conventional encryption techniques:

(i) Unlike traditional encryption schemes that use only integer number fields, chaos-based cryptosystems can be defined by sequence number fields, which include both integer and decimal numbers.

(ii) Digitization of original data for encryption is mandatory for traditional cryptosystems, but it is not required for chaos-based cryptosystems.

(iii) Pseudo-random numbers generated by conventional encryption techniques are periodic, whereas the pseudo-random numbers generated by chaos are non-periodic [39]–[41]. This makes it difficult for attackers to determine the relationship between random numbers to hack the secret keys.

Chaos-based image ciphers are suitable for applications that demand security with minimal execution times. Chaotic ciphers have gained significant popularity due to their high randomness, lower computational complexity, high processing speed, flexibility, and more.

Another promising field involved in the development of image cryptosystems is DNA cryptography [42], [43]. DNA is essentially a biotechnological technique that acts as a repository of vast information. The inherent properties of DNA computing, such as massive storage capacity, immense parallelism, and ultra-low energy consumption, make DNA cryptography an effective add-on component to chaos-based image cryptosystems [44], [45], providing dual-layer security for images in applications that require a higher level of security.

The present study considers the advantages of chaos and DNA cryptography and develops a new chaos and DNA-chaos crypt architecture to meet the security needs of various applications. The following section discusses the focus of the present study.

1.8. Focus of the Present Study

Considering the benefits and drawbacks of existing cryptographic solutions for securing images, the proposed work attempts to develop an image cryptosystem by combining chaos and cryptography to satisfy image security requirements. It takes into account the merits of DNA computing and applies them to design and develop a chaos- and biomolecular-based image cryptosystem. The proposed cryptosystems aim to overcome the challenges of traditional cryptosystems in handling digital images due to the inherent properties of images.

Initially, security algorithms were developed using lower-dimensional chaotic maps. However, lower-dimensional chaotic maps had security flaws due to their key size and limited chaotic range. To overcome this limitation, Chapter 2 discusses the development of fusional chaotic maps that offer better randomness, a higher chaotic range, and larger key sizes. Furthermore, by utilizing the chaotic series generated by this fusional chaotic map, a medical image cryptosystem has been developed in Chapter 3 to achieve better security with a larger key space. The developed fusional chaotic maps are suitable for any size and type of grayscale image, but color image representation differs from grayscale images. Hence, hyperchaotic series are required to provide security for color images.

To address this, Chapter 4 proposes a novel, fast pre-processing hexadecimal technique for generating hyperchaotic series. These chaotic series are then utilized to develop a color image cryptosystem with efficient security. While the hyperchaotic system provides high-end security, some applications require dual-layer security for sensitive images, such as biometric images used as authentication attributes in e-banking and military applications, with minimal computational cost. In response to this requirement, Chapter 5 presents a lightweight integrated crypt architecture by combining chaos and biomolecular computing to enhance the security of biometric images.

All the proposed cryptosystems have been developed using MATLAB 2016a on an Intel(R) Core(TM) i7-6700 CPU @ 3.4 GHz with 16.0 GB RAM running on Windows 8.1 OS. All the proposed image cryptosystems follow the common image cryptosystem architecture, as illustrated in Figure 1.5

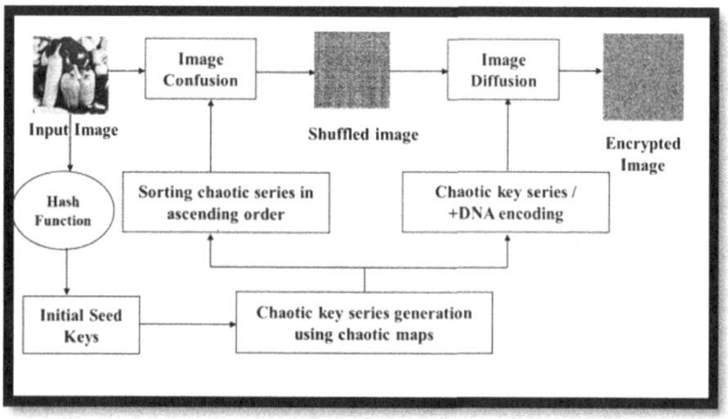

*Figure **Error! No text of specified style in document.**.2 : General Architecture of Chaos and DNA Based Image Cryptosystems*

Step 1: A hash function is applied to the input image to generate the seed key for the chaotic map.
Step 2: The generated seed key is fed as an input to the chaotic map to generate a chaotic key series.
Step 3: The generated chaotic key series is converted into an applicable format and used for the confusion and diffusion of the image.
Step 4: The confusion process is executed based on the index value of the sorted chaotic series to obtain a confused image.
Step 5: The confused image and the applicable integer-format chaotic key series are fed as inputs to the diffusion process. If DNA computing is adopted for encryption, then DNA encoding and DNA encryption are applied during the diffusion process. Finally, the encrypted image is obtained.

To analyze the performance of the developed image encryption algorithms, various analyses such as statistical, differential, keyspace, key sensitivity, cropping attack, noise attack, and complexity analysis were carried out extensively. Statistical analysis was performed using entropy, correlation coefficient, and histogram tests, while differential attacks were evaluated using NPCR and UACI. Various measures such as MSE, PSNR, and SSIM were used to validate the encryption and decryption quality, proving the robustness and effectiveness of the developed cryptosystem.

Based on a detailed analysis of the security requirements for digital images in various applications, and considering the drawbacks of conventional image cryptosystems and the advantages of chaos- and DNA-based cryptosystems, the objective of this research is designed as follows.

1.9. References

i. I.T.R. Center. (2019). *2019 end-of-year data breach report*. Retrieved from https://www.idtheftcenter.org/wpcontent/uploads/2020/01/01.28.2020_ITRC_2019-End-of-Year-Data-Breach-Report_FINAL

ii. IBM. (n.d.). *Data breach.* Retrieved from https://www.ibm.com/security/data-breach

iii. Xu, C., Sun, J., & Wang, C. (2020). A novel image encryption algorithm based on bit-plane matrix rotation and hyper chaotic systems. *Multimedia Tools and Applications,* 79(9–10), 5573–5593. https://doi.org/10.1007/s11042-019-8359-6

iv. Girdhar, A., & Kumar, V. (2018). An RGB image encryption technique using Lorenz and Rossler chaotic systems on DNA sequences. *Multimedia Tools and Applications,* 77(20), 27017–27039. https://doi.org/10.1007/s11042-018-6564-2

v. Talhaoui, M. Z., Wang, X., & Midoun, M. A. (2020). Fast image encryption algorithm with high security level using the Bülban chaotic map. *Journal of Real-Time Image Processing.* https://doi.org/10.1007/s11554-020-00995-x

vi. Alder, S. (2019). *2019 cost of a data breach study: Healthcare data breach costs.* HIPAA Journal. Retrieved fromhttps://www.hipaajournal.com/2019-cost-of-a-data-breach-study-healthcare-data-breach-costs/

vii. New Indian Express. (2020, July 29). Organisations in India lost Rs 14 crore on average to data breaches in August 19 – April 20: IBM. *New Indian Express.* Retrieved from https://www.newindianexpress.com/business/2020/jul/29/organisations-in-india-lost-rs-14-crore-on-average-to-data-breaches-in-august-19--april-20-ibm-2176311.html

viii. Sapkale, Y. (2020). Aadhaar data breach largest in the world, says WEF's Global Risk Report and Avast. *Moneylife*. Retrieved from https://www.moneylife.in/article/aadhaar-data-breach-largest-in-the-world-says-wefs-global-risk-report-and-avast/56384.html

ix. Burt, C. (2020). Biometrics company leaves unhashed fingerprint data of thousands exposed to internet. *Biometric Update*. Retrieved from https://www.biometricupdate.com/202003/biometrics-company-leaves-unhashed-fingerprint-data-of-thousands-exposed-to-internet

x. Security Week. (2020). 70% of IoT devices vulnerable to cyberattacks: HP. *Security Week*. Retrieved from https://www.securityweek.com/70-iot-devices-vulnerable-cyberattacks-hp

xi. Harper, R. (2018). *Note on Naming.*

xii. Wadi, S. M., & Zainal, N. (2014). High definition image encryption algorithm based on AES modification. *Wireless Personal Communications,* 79(2), 811–829. https://doi.org/10.1007/s11277-014-2049-0

xiii. Riaz, F., Hameed, S., Shafi, I., Kausar, R., & Ahmed, A. (2012). Enhanced image encryption techniques using modified advanced encryption standard. *Communications in Computer and Information Science, 281,* 385–396. https://doi.org/10.1007/978-3-642-35883-5_39

xiv. Upadhyay, S., Dave, D., & Sharma, G. (2016). Image encryption by using block-based symmetric transformation algorithm (International Data Encryption Algorithm). *Advances in Intelligent Systems and Computing, 408,* 531–539. https://doi.org/10.1007/978-81-322-2689-4_48

xv. Kumar, M., Sathish, G., Alphonse, M., & Lahcen, R. A. M. (2019). A new RGB image encryption using generalized heat equation associated with generalized Vigenère-type table over symmetric group. *Multimedia Tools and Applications, 78*(19), 27813–27829. https://doi.org/10.1007/s11042-019-7466-4

xvi. Ullagaddi, V., Hassan, F., & Devabhaktuni, V. (2015). Symmetric synchronous stream encryption using images. *Signal, Image and Video Processing, 9*(1), 1–8. https://doi.org/10.1007/s11760-013-0477-x

xvii. Guleria, V., Sabir, S., & Mishra, D. C. (2020). Security of multiple RGB images by RSA cryptosystem combined with FrDCT and Arnold transform. *Journal of Information Security and Applications, 54*, 102542. https://doi.org/10.1016/j.jisa.2020.102542

xviii. Dawahdeh, Z. E., Yaakob, S. N., & Othman, R. R. B. (2018). A new image encryption technique combining Elliptic Curve Cryptosystem with Hill Cipher. *Journal of King Saud University - Computer and Information Sciences, 30*(3), 349–355. https://doi.org/10.1016/j.jksuci.2017.03.014

xix. Ren, G., Han, J., Fu, J., & Shan, M. (2018). Asymmetric image encryption using phase-truncated discrete multiple-parameter fractional Fourier transform. *Optics Review, 25*(6), 701–707. https://doi.org/10.1007/s10043-018-00298-6

xx. Ren, G., Han, J., Fu, J., & Shan, M. (2020). Asymmetric multiple-image interference cryptosystem using discrete cosine transform and conditional decomposition. *Optics Review, 27*(1), 1–8. https://doi.org/10.1007/s10043-019-00420-3

xxi. Abdelfatah, R. I. (2020). Secure image transmission using chaotic-enhanced elliptic curve cryptography. *IEEE Access, 8*, 3875–3890. https://doi.org/10.1109/ACCESS.2020.2975681

xxii. Zhou, K., Fan, J., Fan, H., & Li, M. (2020). Secure image encryption scheme using double random-phase encoding and compressed sensing. *Optics and Laser Technology, 121*, 25–30. https://doi.org/10.1016/j.optlastec.2019.07.021

xxiii. Zhu, S., & Zhu, C. (2019). A new image compression-encryption scheme based on compressive sensing and cyclic shift. *Multimedia Tools and Applications, 78*(15), 20855–20875. https://doi.org/10.1007/s11042-019-7476-2

xxiv. Setyaningsih, E., Wardoyo, R., & Sari, A. K. (2020). Securing color image transmission using compression-encryption model with dynamic key generator and efficient symmetric key distribution. *Digital Communications and Networks, 6*(4), 486–503. https://doi.org/10.1016/j.dcan.2020.02.001

xxv. Cao, C., Sun, K., & Liu, W. (2018). A novel bit-level image encryption algorithm based on 2D-LICM hyperchaotic map. *Multimedia Tools and Applications, 143*, 122–133. https://doi.org/10.1007/s11042-018-6316-6

xxvi. Chen, X. D., Liu, Q., Wang, J., & Wang, Q. H. (2018). Asymmetric encryption of multi-image based on compressed sensing and feature fusion with high quality image reconstruction. *Optics and Laser Technology, 107*, 302–312. https://doi.org/10.1016/j.optlastec.2018.03.029

xxvii. Chai, X., Bi, J., Gan, Z., Liu, X., Zhang, Y., & Chen, Y. (2020). Color image compression and encryption scheme based on compressive sensing and double random encryption strategy. *Signal Processing, 176*, 107567. https://doi.org/10.1016/j.sigpro.2020.107567

xxviii. Krishnamoorthi, R., & Murali, P. (2017). A selective image encryption based on square-wave shuffling with orthogonal polynomials transformation suitable for mobile devices. *Multimedia Tools and Applications, 76*(1), 1217–1246. https://doi.org/10.1007/s11042-016-3753-2

xxix. xxix. Awad, A. I., & Hassaballah, M. (2016). Image feature detectors and descriptors. *Studies in Computational Intelligence, 630*, 203–226. https://doi.org/10.1007/978-3-319-29720-3_13

xxx. Khashan, O. A., & Alshaikh, M. (2020). Edge-based lightweight selective encryption scheme for digital medical images. *Journal of King Saud University - Computer and Information Sciences*. https://doi.org/10.1016/j.jksuci.2020.09.004

xxxi. Gao, H., Gao, T., & Cheng, R. (2016). Random selective image encryption algorithm based on chaos search. *Communications in Computer and Information Science, 634*, 92–105. https://doi.org/10.1007/978-3-319-46056-5_9

xxxii. Shen, Y., Tang, C., Xu, M., & Lei, Z. (2021). Optical selective encryption based on the FRFCM algorithm and face biometric for the medical image. *Optics and Laser Technology, 138*, 106748. https://doi.org/10.1016/j.optlastec.2020.106748

xxxiii. Liu, H., Wen, F., & Kadir, A. (2019). Construction of a new 2D Chebyshev-Sine map and its application to color image encryption. *Multimedia Tools and Applications, 78*(12), 15997–16010. https://doi.org/10.1007/s11042-019-7415-3

xxxiv. xxxiv. Chai, X., Fu, X., Gan, Z., Lu, Y., & Chen, Y. (2019). A color image cryptosystem based on dynamic DNA encryption and chaos. *Multimedia Tools and Applications, 155*, 44–62. https://doi.org/10.1007/s11042-018-6813-6

xxxv. Darwish, S. M. (2019). A modified image selective encryption-compression technique based on 3D chaotic maps and arithmetic coding. *Multimedia Tools and Applications, 78*(14), 19229–19252. https://doi.org/10.1007/s11042-019-7660-4

xxxvi. Ayoup, A. M., Hussein, A. H., & Attia, M. A. A. (2016). Efficient selective image encryption.

Multimedia Tools and Applications, 75(24), 17171–17186. https://doi.org/10.1007/s11042-016-3901-1

xxxvii. Guesmi, R., & Ben Farah, M. A. (2020). A new efficient medical image cipher based on hybrid chaotic map and DNA code. *Journal of King Saud University - Computer and Information Sciences.* https://doi.org/10.1016/j.jksuci.2020.05.009

xxxviii. Faragallah, O. S., et al. (2020). Secure color image cryptosystem based on chaotic logistic in the FrFT domain. *Multimedia Tools and Applications, 79*(3–4), 2495–2519. https://doi.org/10.1007/s11042-019-8254-4

xxxix. François, M., Grosges, T., Barchiesi, D., & Erra, R. (2014). Pseudo-random number generator based on mixing of three chaotic maps. *Communications in Nonlinear Science and Numerical Simulation, 19*, 887–895. https://doi.org/10.1016/j.cnsns.2013.09.029

xl. Ye, G., Zhao, H., & Chai, H. (2016). Chaotic image encryption algorithm using wave-line permutation and block diffusion. *Nonlinear Dynamics, 83*(4), 2067–2077. https://doi.org/10.1007/s11071-015-2577-0

xli. Li, C., Luo, G., Qin, K., & Li, C. (2017). An image encryption scheme based on chaotic tent map. *Nonlinear Dynamics, 87*(1), 127–133. https://doi.org/10.1007/s11071-016-3021-7

xlii. Chai, X., Fu, X., Gan, Z., Lu, Y., & Chen, Y. (2019). A color image cryptosystem based on dynamic DNA encryption and chaos. *Signal Processing, 155*, 44–62. https://doi.org/10.1016/j.sigpro.2018.07.023

xliii. Liu, Y., & Zhang, J. (2020). A multidimensional chaotic image encryption algorithm based on DNA coding. *Multimedia Tools and Applications, 79*(29–30), 21579–21601. https://doi.org/10.1007/s11042-020-09179-7

xliv. Zefreh, E. Z. (2020). An image encryption scheme based on a hybrid model of DNA computing, chaotic systems and hash functions. *Multimedia Tools and Applications, 79*(33–34), 24993–25022.

https://doi.org/10.1007/s11042-020-08501-9

xlv. Wang, Y., Wu, C., Kang, S., Wang, Q., & Mikulovich, V. I. (2020). Multi-channel chaotic encryption algorithm for color image based on DNA coding. *Multimedia Tools and Applications, 79*(25–26), 18317–18342. https://doi.org/10.1007/s11042-020-08959-1

CHAPTER 2
Non-Linear Chaos-Based Image Cryptosystems: A Review

2.1. Chaos System

Consistently achieving effective encryption has always been proven essential in the domain of chaos-based cryptosystems. Defense and intelligence agencies use a wide variety of encryption applications to perform everyday tasks. On the one hand, technology has made the encryption and transmission of images safe and secure, but on the other hand, it has also facilitated the development of advanced interception and cryptanalysis techniques. Encryption keys and codes have become more sophisticated, progressing from simple text substitution ciphers to advanced algorithms composed of large pseudo primes, exponents, and specific consistency.

In any case, the intent and concept of encryption have always remained simple and unchanged—to enable the secure transmission of data from one point to another and prevent all possible chances of unauthorized interception or decoding of data. The advent of the internet has made information freely accessible, while also making data security and protection a major concern for anyone who uses the internet.

The history of chaos-based cryptography spans more than two decades. A small number of primary works were developed in the 1990s; however, it was only in the 2000s that chaotic cryptography reached its peak in terms of popularity and a wider range of applications. Since then, chaotic cryptography has remained a highly popular and dynamic field of research, though with little impact on traditional cryptography.

The use of chaos in cryptography appears very natural, as unique chaotic properties blend with the essential cryptographic qualities of uncertainty and dispersion. This idea of chaos appears in Shannon's works from 1949, much earlier than the term 'chaos' appeared in writings related to cryptography. The deep eccentricity and irregularity of chaotic signals are among the most enticing features of deterministic chaotic systems. These features make chaotic systems highly suitable for novel cryptographic applications. Chaos systems are used to create, reproduce, support, and control other techniques, thereby optimizing the performance of encryption in scientific, engineering, and commercial applications. Turbulent and dynamic frameworks have a point of convergence and give rise to subjectively direct frameworks that create deterministic pseudo-mediation, leading to the execution of efficient cryptography.

2.2. Evolution and Key Characteristics of Chaos Cryptography

In 1963, Edward N. Lorenz discovered chaos theory [1] and described the behavior of chaotic systems as a nonlinear, deterministic dynamic. Chaos is multidisciplinary and has applications in fields such as Mathematics, Physics, Communications, Meteorology, and Biomedicine. Since the 1990s, researchers have identified a close interrelationship between chaos and cryptology. They found that many characteristics of chaotic functions have specific counterparts in conventional cryptosystems [2], [3]. Table 2.1

shows the interrelationship and variance that exist between chaos and cryptology [4], [5].

Chaos Theory	Cryptology
Chaotic map used for encryption	Algorithm used for encryption
Sensitivity to initial condition	Key-dependent confusion and diffusion
Iterative process	Multi-round transformation
System parameters act as a key	No system parameters act as a key
Prime numbers not required	Prime numbers are required
Involves floating point arithmetic	Involves integer arithmetic
Based on any non-linear function	Based on mod function

Table 2.1: Relationships and Variations between Chaos Theory and Cryptology

Due to the close correlation between chaos and cryptology, chaotic maps are widely used in the encryption process. The three ways of using chaos theory in encryption schemes are:

i. Chaotic maps are used to generate chaotic key sequences, which are used as pseudo-random bytes or numbers with desirable mathematical properties for key generation.
ii. The generated chaotic key values are utilized to confuse images.
iii. In the cryptosystem, the diffusion process is executed using an acceptable integer form of the generated chaotic key series.

In mathematics, a chaotic map is seen as an evolution function that defines some sort of chaotic behavior. A chaotic map is also a discrete-time dynamic system [6]–[8]. In chaos-based image cryptosystems, chaotic maps are used to generate chaotic sequences, which are used for permutation and substitution [9]–[12]. Chaotic maps are categorized into different forms, such as: One-Dimensional (1D) chaotic maps generate one chaotic sequence, Two-

Dimensional (2D) chaotic maps generate two chaotic series, and three-dimensional and four-dimensional chaotic maps generate their corresponding number of chaotic series.

2.3. Survey of Chaos-Based Image Encryption Techniques

In the past decade, the significance and use of images in social media, key industrial sectors, and medical applications have increased tremendously. Following this trend, the need to maintain the privacy and secrecy of sensitive images while being transmitted over insecure networks has become essential. Traditional encryption techniques such as ElGamal schemes, AES, and DES [13] are not effective in encrypting digital images due to the inherent qualities of images, such as high data capacity, high correlation between pixels, and high redundancy, which render them inefficient in many ways [14]–[16]. Therefore, researchers feel a huge need to develop efficient and fast image cryptosystems to encrypt digital images.

To overcome the limitations of traditional encryption techniques, different methodologies of image encryption have been developed. Among them, chaos-based image encryption is preferable for all types and sizes of images [17]–[21]. Chaos-based cryptosystems have several merits over conventional encryption techniques in many aspects [22], [23], including security, computational overhead, time, and speed complexity. Figure 2.1 shows the inherent properties of chaos systems, making them highly desirable for use in image cryptosystems.

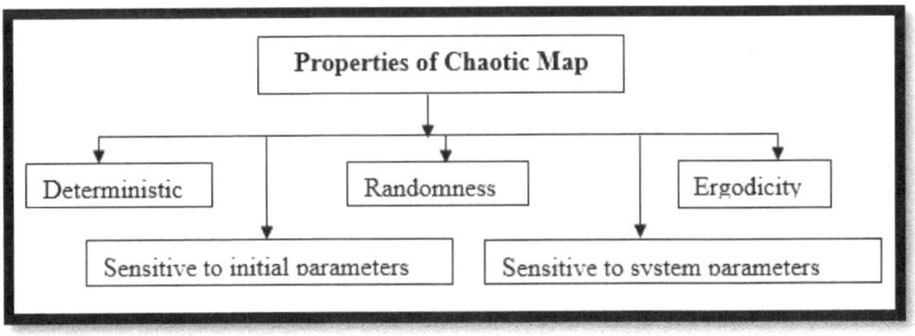

*Figure **Error! No text of specified style in document.**.3 : Basic Inherent Properties of Chaotic Systems*

Specifically, in chaotic systems, a key series includes integer and decimal numbers, and the digitization of an image is not required for the encryption process. Moreover, pseudo-random numbers generated by chaotic functions are non-periodic.

As illustrated in Figure 2.2, chaos-based image cipher architecture is divided into two phases [24]–[26]: chaotic series-based permutation and substitution. In the permutation phase, pixel positions of the original image are shuffled depending on the chaotic sequence index delivered by the chaotic functions [27]. Permutation alone will not provide maximum security for images because the histogram of the plain image and the shuffled image remain the same and are vulnerable to statistical attacks. Therefore, substitution acts as a main component in image ciphers. In the substitution phase, each pixel value of the image is converted into another value using the sequence generated by the chaotic system. After the substitution phase, the histogram of the original image and the substituted image is entirely different. Therefore, substitution yields better security compared to permutation. To achieve reasonable security for images, both permutation and substitution must be used in the image encryption process [28].

Chaos-based image ciphers are employed in applications where high computational complexity with minimal execution time is required. Consequently, these chaotic ciphers have gained popularity due to their high randomness, computational complexity, high processing speed, and flexibility. Recent studies on chaotic systems focus on designing efficient chaos-based image cryptosystems with reduced execution time for use in biometric applications [29], [30], medical applications [31], [32], and secure image-based satellite communication [33], [34]. The overall objective of the present chapter is to highlight the significance of chaos-based image ciphers and to survey different chaos techniques used for enhancing the security of images.

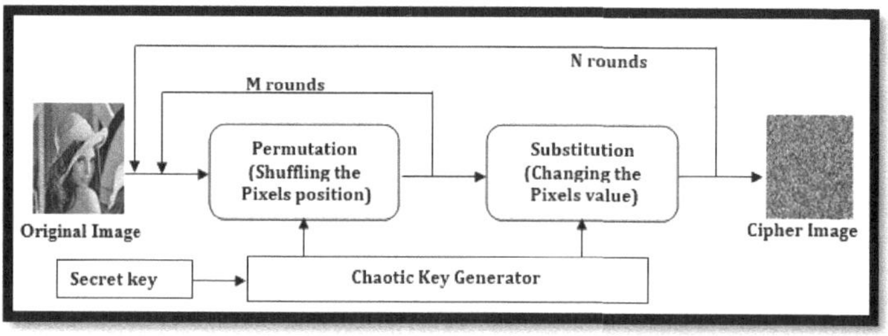

Figure 2.2: Architecture of Image Encryption

2.3.1. Methodologies of Image Encryption Using 1D Chaotic Map

Many image encryption schemes using different 1D chaotic maps have been proposed in the literature. Figure. 2.3 illustrate different types of 1D chaotic map used in image cryptosystem. The simplicity and randomness of 1D chaotic maps have attracted many researchers. Various image cryptosystem has been proposed by using 1D chaotic maps.

The simplest form of 1D chaotic map is a logistic map, which is used to implement permutation process in image encryption. It primarily focuses on scrambling the pixels using a random sequence generated by 1D logistic map. [35], [36]. The major observation on the result of 1D logistic map shows the resemblance set of chaotic sequence, so it reflects less security on image encryption. Tent map is another familiar 1D map [37], which is used in many image cryptosystems.

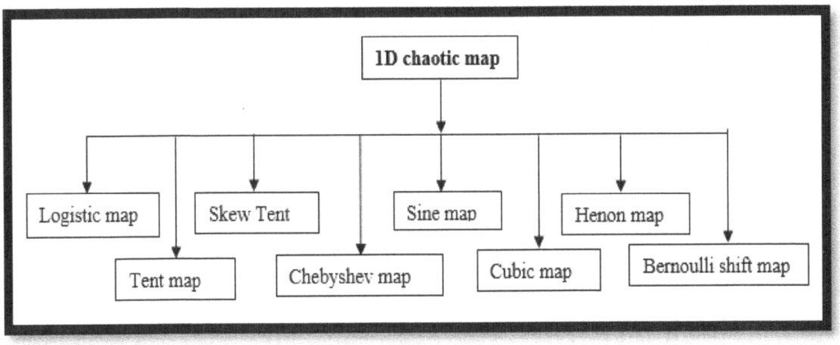

Figure 2.3: Different Types of One Dimensional Chaotic Map

Medina *et al.* [38] proved that the random sequence generated by the tent map has more chaotic behavior than the logistic map. However, in both logistic and tent maps, only one input parameter is used as a key to generate the chaotic sequences. So, the key size is small, which is vulnerable to brute force attack. To overcome this problem, an advanced version of tent map known as skew tent map is proposed [39]. The skew tent map has two input parameters to produce random sequences and offers higher chaotic behavior. Kadir *et al.* proposed image encryption using the skew tent map to generate the chaotic sequence for permutation process and obtained good encryption results [40]. Zhou *et al.* proposed three different chaotic systems by combining logistic map and tent map to obtain higher chaotic behavior, those chaotic maps are used in both permutation process and also substitution process of image encryption [41]. Another map, which has excellent properties of pseudo random generator is Chebyshev map [42]. The chaotic sequences generated by this map are orthogonal polynomial sequences with higher entropy values. As stated by "Shannon's theory of perfect-security", the keys used for encryption must be produced randomly with a high level of entropy. So the Chebyshev map provides high level of security for images. The different form of 1D chaotic map is Henon map [10], it uses two parameters to generate the chaotic sequence, and also it uses feedback process for calculating the next chaotic sequence value. The chaotic behavior of the Henon map is comparatively higher than all the other 1D chaotic maps as all other 1D maps use only one previous value to calculate the next chaotic key. Even though Henon map has comparatively higher chaotic behavior, it suffers from computation function used to generate chaotic sequences, which is simple and vulnerable to statistical attack. The alternative methodology for producing chaotic behavior is "stretch and fold" mechanism using Bernoulli shift map [43]. There are some effective dynamical structures in generalized Bernoulli shift maps, such as desired auto-correlation and cross-correlation, so it provides good image encryption effect [44].

[ref.]	1D chaotic map	Governing equation	Parameter range	Correlation test	Merits
[46]	Logistic map	$x_n = \alpha x_{n-1}(1 - x_{n-1})$	$3.5 \leq \alpha \leq 4$	-0.8330	simplest form of chaotic map
[37,] [38]	Tent map	$x_{n+1} = \begin{cases} \mu x_n/2 & x_n < 0.5 \\ \mu(1 - x_n)/2 & 0.5 \leq x_n \end{cases}$	$0 \leq \mu \leq 4$	-0.4322	Insensitive to initial value
[39],[40], [47]	Skew tent map	$f(x) = \begin{cases} x/p & if\ x \in [0, p] \\ (1 - x)/(1 - p) & if\ x \in [p, 1] \end{cases}$	$0 \leq x \leq 1$	0.5423	Always have positive Lyapunov exponent
[41]	Sine map	$x_{n+1} = \alpha\, sin(\pi x_n)/4$	$0 \leq \alpha \leq 4$	-0.0771	More uniform distribution of random numbers
[42]	Chebyshav map	$z_{i+1} = \cos(w \cos^{-1} z_i)$	$2 \leq w \leq 6$	-0.0061	Dynamics are orthogonal polynomial sequences
[48]	Cubic map	$x_{n+1} = \mu x_n^3 + (1 - \mu)x_n$	$3.2 \leq \mu \leq 4$	-0.1493	Simple nature easy to implement
[49]	Henon map	$x_n = 1 + \lambda(x_{n-2} - x_{n-3}) + \alpha x_{n-2}^2$	$\lambda=3$, $1.07 \leq \alpha \leq 1.09$	0.9997	Use two control parameters, increased key size
[43], [50], [51]	Bernoulli shift map	$x_{n+1} = \begin{cases} 2x_n, & if\ x_n \in [0, 1/2] \\ 2x_n - 1, & if\ x_n \in [1/2, 1] \end{cases}$	$0 \leq x_n \leq 1$	0.0208	Yield nonlinear "stretch and cut "mechanism to generate deterministic chaos.

Table ***Error! No text of specified style in document.****.1 : Summarization of the Governing Equations, Parameter Range, Randomness and Merits of 1D Chaotic Maps*

Owing to their desirable characteristics, chaotic maps have become popular among cryptography researchers. Following this trend, many researchers have proposed new 1D chaotic maps and achieved optimal encryption of images. Table 2.2 discusses some of the key 1D chaotic maps, along with their mathematical expressions, parameter ranges, and correlation test results, to determine the chaotic behavior of the random numbers generated by different 1D chaotic maps. It also discusses the merits of each map. Figure 2.3 illustrates the permutation process of an image using a 1D logistic map. Using a chaotic sequence, confusion is performed by swapping the positions of pixels either in the vertical or horizontal direction of the image. Figure 2.4 (b) and (c) show the permutation outcome of the Lena image.

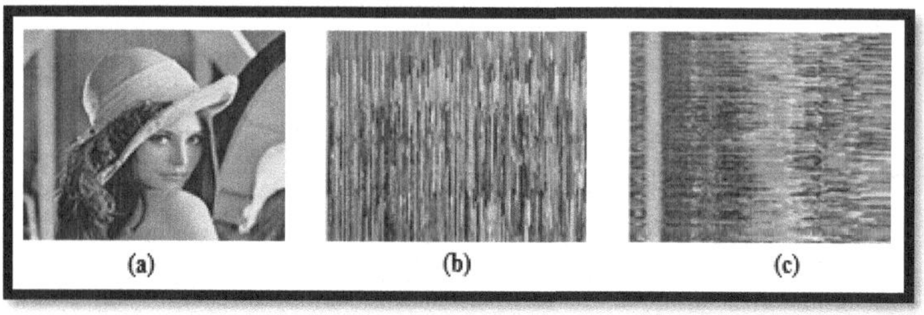

Figure 2.4: Transposition Using 1D Logistic Map
A) Original Image B) Vertical Transposition C) Horizontal Transposition

The chaotic behavior of the sequences generated by the 1D chaotic maps is limited because redundancy of chaotic sequence occurred after particular range, so it is effective only for encrypting small size images. Initial values and system parameter of chaotic maps are considered as a keys for generating the chaotic series, but the range of these keys are restricted to limited values. Hence, the key size also very small and vulnerable to brute force attack [45]. The complexity of the chaotic evolution function is simple, and so it cannot resist statistical attack. To overcome these limitations, 2D chaotic maps were invented with large key space. The 2D chaotic maps use more than two system parameters, and initial values are used as a seed key to generate the chaotic sequence. This increases the complexity of the chaotic system and makes image cryptosystem attacks nearly impossible.

2.3.2. Methodologies of Image Ciphers Using 2D Chaotic Maps

Limitations of 1D chaotic systems led to the evolution of 2D chaotic systems. In the 1D chaotic map based image cryptosystem, rows and columns of the image are shuffled separately with compromising the execution time, so the time required for confusing the image is high. In 2D chaotic map based image encryption, both rows and columns of the image are shuffled simultaneously, and the time required for shuffling is less when compared to 1D chaotic based image ciphers. Figure 2.5 shows some of the common 2D chaotic maps used for image encryption.

The development of 2D chaotic maps with robust security features encouraged researchers to use different 2D chaotic maps for securing images. In the earlier stages, they created 2D chaotic maps by combining two 1D chaos functions. Based on this principle, two-coupled logistic maps [45] have been proposed to generate two different chaotic sequences to confuse and diffuse the image.

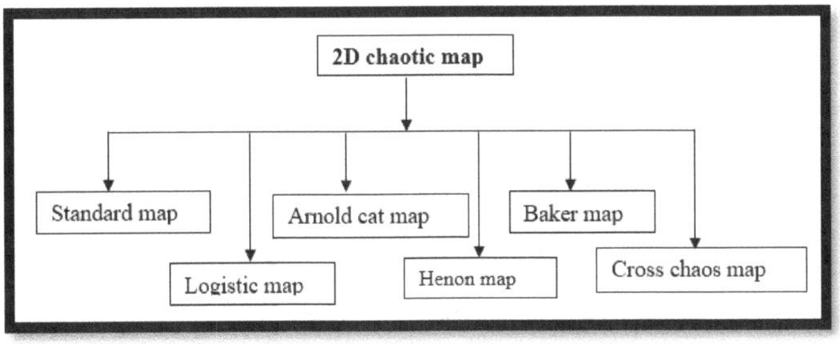

Figure 2.5: Different Types of 2D Chaotic Map

With the prevalent use of 2D chaotic maps in the field of image cryptosystems, unique 2D chaotic functions have been proposed without utilizing the existing 1D chaotic maps. Anil Kumar et al. [52] generated a synthetic image using a 2D standard map; this synthetic image is taken as a key image and used for encrypting the original image. Osama et al. reported an efficient chaotic-based image cryptosystem using an enhanced 2D standard map [53]. Vinod Patidar et al. combined a 1D logistic map and a 2D standard map to generate chaotic key streams for confusing and diffusing the images [54]. Another good random behavior chaotic map is the 2D logistic map, an expanded form of the 1D logistic map [55]. The chaotic sequence generated by the 2D logistic map has higher chaotic behavior and helps to increase the complexity of the confusion process in image ciphers. It has six seed keys for generating the chaotic key series; a small variation in these keys leads to a dramatic change in the result of decryption [56]. This makes it challenging to apply an exhaustive attack to obtain the original image. In addition to these maps, the Arnold cat map is one of the most discrete systems that provide higher chaotic behavior. In most image cryptosystems, the Arnold cat map is used to generate new index values to shuffle the pixels of an image [57], [58].

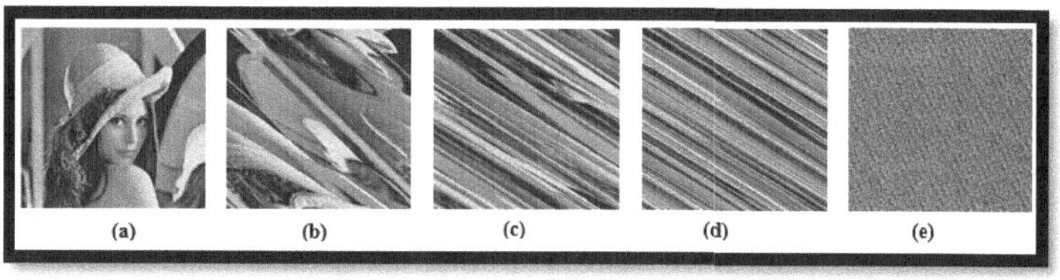

Figure 2.6: Image Confusion (a) Original image (b) Result of first iteration of confusion (c) Output of second iteration (d) Output of second iteration (e) Final confused image after tenth iteration

Figure 2.6 shows a sample confusion process in image encryption based on swapping the pixel position based on key value generated by Arnold cat map for ten iterations.

2D Henon map is another widely used chaotic map [59]. Tong *et al.* proved that the 2D Henon map has high pseudo random features and generates chaotic sequences at higher speeds when compared to logistic map [60]. Baker map, an extension of the Tent map, is a 2D chaotic map, mainly employed in image cryptosystems to change the sequence of pixel positions [61]. It breaks an image into different parts by rearranging the parts during the confusion phase. Discretized baker map, another version of the Baker map [62], uses secret key for deciding the number of divisions in an image. If the secret key contains k elements, then the image is separated into k upright rectangles. Firstly, the image with dimensions N × N is separated into k upright rectangles of altitude N and width is N_i ($0 < i < k$). Then, the vertically sliced image is converted into horizontal slices, and each horizontal slice of the image is placed from bottom to top. The final result of this process is a confused image, which is ready for further process of encryption. One of the chaotic map functions that use high mathematical computation to generate the chaotic sequence is a cross chaotic map. Many researchers analysed the cross chaotic map and proved that it has high chaos complexity than logistic chaotic maps [63], [64]. Table 2.3 summarizes different 2D chaotic maps with their mathematical expression, key value, and system parameter range and number of keys used for image encryption.

[ref]	2D chaotic map	Governing equations	Initial values and parameters range	No. of keys
[54]	Standard map	$X_{n+1} = (X_n + K\ sinY_n)\ mod\ 2\pi$ $Y_{n+1} = (Y_n + X_{n+1})mod\ 2\pi$	$0 < X_i, Y_i < 2\pi$ $K > 0$	3 (x_0, y_0, K)
[55]	Logistic map	$x_{i+1} = \mu_1 x_i(1 - x_i) + \gamma_1 y_i^2$ $y_{i+1} = \mu_2 y_i(1 - y_i) + \gamma_2(x_i^2 + x_i y_i)$	$2.75 < \mu_1, \mu_2 \leq 3.45$ $0.15 < \gamma_1, \gamma_2 \leq 0.21$ $0 < x_i, y_i < 1$	6 $(x_0, y_0, \mu_1, \mu_2, \gamma_1, \gamma_2)$
[52]	Arnold cat map	$\begin{bmatrix} x' \\ y' \end{bmatrix} = \begin{bmatrix} 1 & p \\ q & pq+1 \end{bmatrix} \begin{bmatrix} x \\ y \end{bmatrix} mod\ N$	N = width/ height of square image. X and Y are pixel positions and p,q>0	4 (p, q, x_0, y_0)
[59]	Henon map	$\begin{cases} x_{d+1} = y_d + 1 - a x_d^2 \\ y_{d+1} = b x_d \end{cases}$	$a = 1.40, b = 0.2$ $0 < x_i, y_i < 1$	2 (x_0, y_0)
[61]	Baker map	$B(x, y) = \left(2x, \frac{y}{2}\right), \quad 0 \leq x < \frac{1}{2}$ $B(x, y) = \left(2x - 1, \frac{y}{2} + \frac{1}{2}\right), \quad \frac{1}{2} \leq x < 1$	X and y are the position of pixels in image	2 (x_0, y_0)
[63]	Cross chaotic map	$\begin{cases} x_i = sin^2\left(3arcsin\sqrt{\lvert y_{i-1}\rvert}\right) \\ y_i = 4x_{i-1}^3 - 3x_{i-1} \end{cases}$	$0 < x_i, y_i < 1$	2 (x_0, y_0)

Table 2.3: Summarization of the Governing Equations and Parameter Range of 2d Chaotic Map

2.3.3. Methodologies of Image Ciphers Using Higher Dimensional (HD) Chaotic Maps

Most of the 1D- and 2D-based image cryptosystems produce satisfactory results. However, as specified by Zheng et al. [56], lower-dimensional chaotic systems suffer from two major drawbacks: a limited range of random chaotic series and a lower key space, which is insufficient to resist brute-force attacks. Mondal et al. [65] remarked that a few initial seed keys can be easily estimated, and the less complex structure of lower-dimensional map-based cryptosystems makes them vulnerable to statistical attacks. Many lower-dimensional image cryptosystems have been cryptanalyzed [66], [67]. Higher-dimensional chaotic maps overcome these drawbacks through their desirable features, such as higher randomness, longer periodicity, and a higher range of positive Lyapunov exponents [68], [69]. The familiar three-dimensional chaotic map is Chen's chaotic map, designed by Chen in 1999. Many researchers found that Chen's chaotic system can be implemented easily in circuits and has optimal dynamical properties needed for cryptosystems [70]. Jun-Xin Chen et al. proposed a new image cipher using Chen's map for image permutation [71]. Chen's chaotic map sequences exhibit high randomness that persists for a longer duration [72]. This property makes it suitable for encrypting images of large sizes. This map has sufficient randomness, as the correlation between each value in the sequence is significantly low. Further, Chen proposed a new four-dimensional chaotic map known as the hyper-chaotic map, which generates four different chaotic series [73] by using eight input parameters, resulting in a comparatively higher key space and adequate robustness to resist statistical attacks.

Similar to Chen's chaotic system, Lorenz discovered a new chaotic map known as the Lorenz 3D chaotic map [74], [75], which generates three chaotic series (X, Y, Z), and their attractors are disclosed in Figure 2.7. It is clear that the chaotic sequence generated by the Lorenz map has high randomness. Lorenz extended the three-dimensional chaotic map to a four-dimensional chaotic map, which has the same features as Chen's hyper-chaotic system [76].

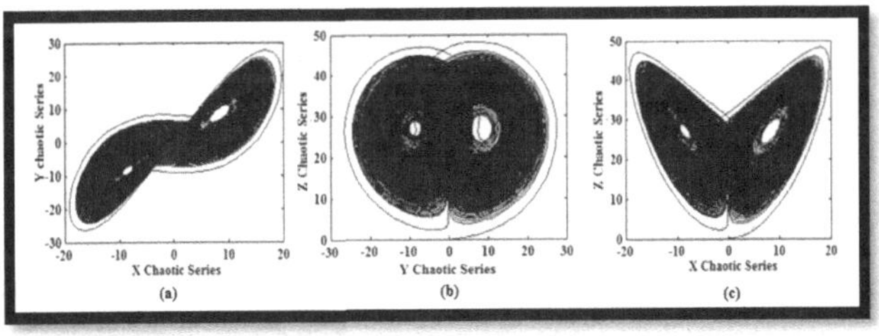

Figure 2.7: Chaos Attractors of Lorenz Map (A) X-Y Plane (B) Y-Z Plane (C) X-Z Plane

[ref]	2D chaotic map	Governing equations	Initial values and parameters range	No. of keys
[71]	3D chen's chaotic map	$\dot{x} = a(y - x)$ $\dot{y} = (c - a)x - xz + cy$ $\dot{z} = x\dot{y} - bz$	$a = 35, b = 3, c = 28$	3 (x_0, y_0, z_0)
[73]	4D chen's hyper chaotic map	$\dot{x} = a(y - x)$ $\dot{y} = -xy + dx + cy - q$ $\dot{z} = xy - bz$ $\dot{q} = x + k$	$a = 36, b = 3$ $c = 28, d = 16$ $-0.7 \leq k \leq 0.7$	5 (x_0, y_0, z_0, q_0)
[74], [75]	3D Loren chaotic map	$\dot{x} = a(y - x)$ $\dot{y} = cx - y - xz$ $\dot{z} = xy - bz$	$a = 10, b = \frac{8}{3}, c = 28$	3 (x_0, y_0, z_0)
[76]	4D Lorenz hyper chaotic system	$\dot{x} = a(y - x) + w$ $\dot{y} = cx \dot{-} y - xz$ $\dot{z} = x\dot{y} - bz$ $\dot{w} = -\dot{y}z + rw$	$a = 10, b = \frac{8}{3}, c = 28$ $-1.53 < r \leq -0.06$	5 (x_0, y_0, z_0, w_0, r)
[77]	3D Rössler hyper chaotic system	$x_1(k+1) = \alpha x_1(k)\big(1 - x_1(k)\big) - \beta(x_3(k) + \gamma(1 - 2x$ $x_2(k+1) = \delta x_1(k)\big(1 - x_1(k)\big) + cx_3(k)$ $x_1(k+1) = ((x_3(k) + \gamma)(1 - 2x_2(k) - 1)\big(1 - \theta x_1(k)$	$\alpha = 3.8, \beta = 0.05,$ $\gamma = 3.78, c = 0.2,$ $n = 0.1, \theta = 1.9$ $x(0) = (0.3, 0, 0.05)$	3 $(x1_0, x2_0, x3_0)$

Table 2.4: Summarization of the Governing Equations and Parameter Range of 2D Chaotic Map

The Rossler chaotic map, a recently developed three-dimensional chaotic map [77], exhibits the same chaotic behavior as other three-dimensional chaotic systems. The chaotic sequence generated by this map is utilized for the confusion and diffusion process to achieve a good biometric image encryption algorithm. Kanso et al. developed a new three-dimensional Arnold cat map by borrowing the properties of the 2D Arnold cat map [78]. Many researchers have used three- and four-dimensional chaotic functions to encrypt color images because a color image has three components—RGB (Red, Green, Blue)—so each separate chaotic series generated by these chaotic systems is utilized for encrypting each component separately [79].

2.4. Performance Evaluation Metrics

Various evaluation metrics used to analyze the performance and security of chaos-based image cryptosystems are discussed in the following sections.

2.4.1. Benchmark Evaluation Metrics of Image Cryptosystems

It is essential to evaluate the security and robustness of newly developed image cryptosystems. This section discusses the commonly used benchmark performance and security analyses to determine the level of security of chaos-based image cryptosystems.

2.4.2. Statistical Analysis

The main aim of image cryptosystems is to convert a meaningful input image into a noisy image. During the transmission of the image over an insecure network, noisy images might be intercepted by cryptanalysts. Decoders may attempt to break the cryptosystem by identifying numerical relationships between neighboring pixels of the noisy image. They can easily recover the original image once the pixel interrelationship is identified. Hence, a good image cryptosystem should be able to withstand this type of statistical attack. This can be analyzed using three different methods: histogram analysis, correlation coefficient analysis, and entropy analysis. The following section briefly describes these three analyses.

2.4.3. Histogram Analysis

Histogram analysis displays the scattering of pixels in a graphical form [80]. The randomness of the image cryptosystem is determined by the uniform scattering of pixel values in the cipher image. Figure 2.8 depicts the histograms of the original and cipher images. Based on analysis and comparison, the histogram results show that the intensity values of the final encrypted image are uniformly scattered.

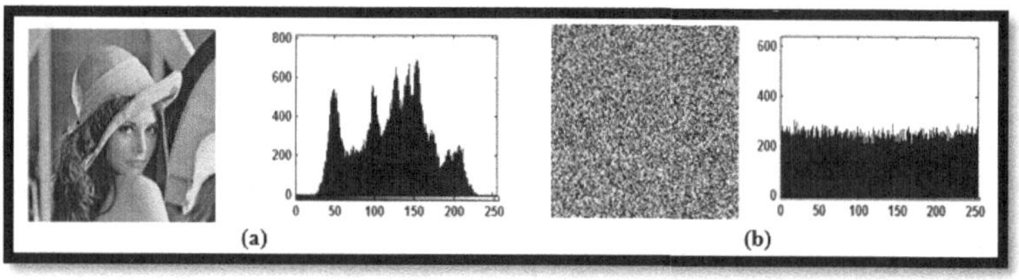

Figure 2.8: Histogram of (a) Original image (b) Cipher image

2.4.4. Correlation Coefficient Analysis

Correlation coefficient (CC) analysis is one of the most efficient ways to determine the robustness of an image cryptosystem [80]. It helps calculate the correlation among neighboring pixels. All adjacent pixels are highly interconnected in the plain image. The main aim of the cryptosystem is to minimize such associations among the pixels and obtain the correlation results of cipher images as zero or as close to zero as possible. The following equation (2.1) is used to compute the correlation coefficients in three directions—horizontal, vertical, and diagonal—of the encrypted and the original image.

$$r_{pq} = \frac{\mathrm{cov}(p,q)}{\sqrt{D(p)}\times\sqrt{D(q)}} \qquad (2.1)$$

Where $\mathrm{Cov}(p,q) = \frac{1}{N}\sum_{i=0}^{n}(p_i - E(p))(q_i - E(q))$

$D(p) = \frac{1}{N}\sum_{i=0}^{n}(p_i - E(q))^2$

$E(p) = \frac{1}{N}\sum_{i=0}^{n} p_i$

Where p and q are the values of two neighboring pixels, Cov (p,q) denotes the covariance, D(p) represents variance, E(p) is the mean value and n/N is the number of pixels. In order to determine the security level of the encryption algorithm, the correlation between the pixel values in all three directions must be obtained. If the correlation between pixel values of the cipher image is lower, then the security level is higher. The ideal value of correlation is 0. If cipher image correlation is 0 or nearest to 0, then it can be concluded that the developed cryptosystem is robust enough to resist statistical analysis.

2.4.1.1. Information Entropy Analysis

This analysis is used to determine the level of pixel randomness in a cipher image [81]. Equation (2.2) stated below describes the calculation of global Shannon information entropy.

$$H(m) = \sum_{i=0}^{M-1} p(m_i)log_2\frac{1}{p(m_i)} \quad (2.2)$$

where m denotes the intensity of the cipher image, and p(m) signifies the probability of the pixel values. The entropy result of the chaotic image is 8. An effective image cryptosystem must offer an entropy result that is closer to 8. However, the global entropy does not quantify the actual randomness of an encrypted image. Wu *et al.* [39] specified three flaws of global entropy — inexactness, instability, and inefficiency. To overcome such shortcomings, they invented a novel metric known as Local Shannon Entropy (LSE). In LSE, exact randomness is computed using the simple average of Shannon entropy of non-overlapped cipher image blocks.

2.4.1.2. Differential Attack Analysis

The common criteria used to identify the sensitivity of the cipher image are NPCR and UACI [82]. The high sensitivity of the encrypted image related to tiny changes in the original image is generally required to prevent differential cryptanalysis. If changes occurred in a single pixel of the plain image, it produces major changes in the ciphered image. This makes it difficult for the adversary to apply chosen plaintext attack. The NPCR and UACI can be defined by the following Equations. (2.3 and 2.4).

$$NPCR = \frac{\sum_{i,j} D(i,j)}{M \times N} \times 100\ \% \quad \text{Where} \quad D(i,j) = \begin{cases} 1, C(i,j) \neq C(i,j), \\ 0, otherwise, \end{cases} \qquad (2.3)$$

$$UACI = \frac{1}{M \times N}\left[\sum_{i,j} \frac{|C(i,j) - C'(i,j)|}{255}\right] \times 100\% \qquad (2.4)$$

Here, M and N represent the height and width of the original image; C and C' represent two cipher images related to the two plain images with single pixel value difference. The average NPCR and UACI values of random images are 99.61 and 33.46, respectively. If the NPCR and UACI values produced by an encryption scheme are very close to these average values, then it can be concluded that the proposed image cipher technique has high sensitivity to plain text attacks and has the robustness to resist differential attacks

2.4.2. Key Space and Key Sensitivity Analysis

One of the most essential aspects of designing any encryption algorithm is the selection of a secret key, as an algorithm's strength is determined by the strength of its secret key [82]. The secret key should have two basic characteristics— a larger key space and high sensitivity. It is extremely difficult for a cryptanalyst to execute an exhaustive or dictionary attack if the key space is large. Apart from the key size, key sensitivity is an essential element in building a cryptosystem. A robust image cipher should be highly sensitive to secret keys. A small change in the secret key set produces an entirely different cipher image. Hence, key sensitivity analysis is crucial, as some parts of the original image can be identified from the detected cipher image by guessing certain exact partial keys.

2.4.3. Evaluation Metrics of Encryption and Decryption Quality

A high-quality image cryptosystem produces a completely different cipher image and an almost identical deciphered image. Both objective and subjective methods are preferred for quality analysis [83]. Objective methods, such as CC, MSE, and PSNR, are based on numerical comparisons between the original and the encrypted/decrypted images. Since objective methods are simple, they are easier to implement than subjective methods. CC is determined using Equation (2.1), while MSE and PSNR are computed using Equations (2.5) and (2.6).

Even though these methods effectively analyze quality, they are inconsistent with the Human Visual System (HVS). The subjective method uses HVS to measure image quality. Various HVS models have been proposed for evaluating an image cryptosystem. Among them, SSIM provides better results than other quality metrics, as it incorporates information about luminance, structure, and contrast to determine image quality. The SSIM result ranges from [-1, 1]. A maximum value of 1 indicates that both the original and cipher images are identical, whereas the minimum value indicates that the cipher image is completely different from the original image. The evaluation of SSIM is expressed in Equation (2.7).

$$MSE = \frac{1}{M \times N} \sum_{i=1}^{M} \sum_{j=1}^{N} (O(i,j) - D/E(i,j))^2 \quad (2.5)$$

$$PSNR = 20 \log_{10} \frac{I_{max}}{\sqrt{MSE}} \quad (2.6)$$

$$SSIM(O, D/E) = \frac{(2\mu_I \mu_C + c_1)(2\sigma_{IC} + c_2)}{(\mu_I^2 + \mu_C^2 + c_1)(\sigma_I^2 + \sigma_C^2 + c_2)} \quad (2.7)$$

Here, O represents the original image, D/E represents Decrypted/Encrypted image; Imax specifies the maximum intensity value of the image; μ_I and μ_C represent the average values; σ_I^2, σ_C^2 are the variance of O, D/E; σ_{IC} is the covariance of O and D/E and c_1 and c_2 are smaller constants. These metrics have been used in different cryptosystems for analysing encryption and decryption quality.

2.4.4. Key Space and Key Sensitivity Analysis

One of the most essential aspects of designing any encryption algorithm is the selection of a secret key, as an algorithm's strength is determined by the strength of its secret key [82]. The secret key should have two basic characteristics— a larger key space and high sensitivity. It is extremely difficult for a cryptanalyst to execute an exhaustive or dictionary attack if the key space is large. Apart from the key size, key sensitivity is an essential element in building a cryptosystem. A robust image cipher should be highly sensitive to secret keys. A small change in the secret key set produces an entirely different cipher image. Hence, key sensitivity analysis is crucial, as some parts of the original image can be identified from the detected cipher image by guessing certain exact partial keys.

2.4.5. Evaluation Metrics of Encryption and Decryption Quality

A high-quality image cryptosystem produces a completely different cipher image and an almost identical deciphered image. Both objective and subjective methods are preferred for quality analysis [83]. Objective methods, such as CC, MSE, and PSNR, are based on numerical comparisons between the original and the encrypted/decrypted images. Since objective methods are simple, they are easier to implement than subjective methods. CC is determined using Equation (2.1), while MSE and PSNR are computed using Equations (2.5) and (2.6).

Even though these methods effectively analyze quality, they are inconsistent with the Human Visual System (HVS). The subjective method uses HVS to measure image quality. Various HVS models have been proposed for evaluating an image cryptosystem. Among them, SSIM provides better results than other quality metrics, as it incorporates information about luminance, structure, and contrast to determine image quality. The SSIM result ranges from [-1, 1]. A maximum value of 1 indicates that both the original and cipher images are identical, whereas the minimum value indicates that the cipher image is completely different from the original image. The evaluation of SSIM is expressed in Equation (2.7).

2.5. *References*

i. Motter, A. E., & Campbell, D. K. (2013). Chaos at fifty. *Physics Today, 66*(5), 27–33.
ii. Kapoor, V. (2003). Chaos and cryptography. *IEEE Transactions on Circuits and Systems I: Fundamental Theory and Applications,* 0(12), 1498–1509.
iii. Jakimoski, G., & Kocarev, L. (2001). Chaos and cryptography: Block encryption ciphers based on chaotic maps. *IEEE Transactions on Circuits and Systems I: Fundamental Theory and Applications, 48*(2), 163–169.
iv. Blackledge, J. M. (2010). Cryptography using chaos: What is the problem? *Technology*, 00–13.
v. Hassani, E., & Eshghi, M. (2013). Image encryption based on chaotic tent map in time and frequency. *International Journal of Computer Applications,* 5(1), 97–110.

vi. Eyebe Fouda, J. S. A., Effa, J. Y., Kom, M., & Ali, M. (2013). The three-state test for chaos detection in discrete maps. *Applied Soft Computing Journal, 13*(12), 4731–4737.

vii. Feng, M., & Liu, J. (2012). Procedia Engineering.

viii. Campos-Cantón, E., Femat, R., & Pisarchik, A. N. (2011). A family of multimodal dynamic maps. *Communications in Nonlinear Science and Numerical Simulation, 16*(9), 3457–3462.

ix. Mori, M. (2001). Pseudo-random sequences generated by piecewise linear maps from the viewpoint of dynamical systems. *Mathematics and Computers in Simulation, 55*(1–3), 177–189.

x. Fan, Z., Xiao-jian, T., Jing-yi, S., & Xue-yan, L. (2008). Pseudo-random sequence generator based on the generalized Henon map. *Chinese Journal of Electronics, 15*(September), 64–68.

xi. Suneel, M. (2009). Cryptographic pseudo-random sequences from the chaotic Henon map. *International Journal of Computational Mathematics, 34*(October), 689–701.

xii. (2008). Pseudo-random bit generation based on 2D chaotic maps of logistic type and its applications. *Nonlinear Dynamics*, 784–796.

xiii. Stallings, W. (2011). *Cryptography and Network Security* (Vol. 139, No. 3).

xiv. Wang, X., & Zhang, H. (2015). A novel image encryption algorithm based on genetic recombination and hyper-chaotic systems. *Nonlinear Dynamics, Online*(1), 333–346.

xv. Wang, X., Liu, C., & Zhang, H. (2016). An effective and fast image encryption algorithm based on chaos and interweaving of ranks. *Nonlinear Dynamics, 84*(3), 1595–1607.

xvi. Hu, G., Xiao, D., Zhang, Y., & Xiang, T. (2017). An efficient chaotic image cipher with dynamic lookup table driven bit-level permutation strategy. *Nonlinear Dynamics, 87*(2), 1359–1375.

xvii. Ji, X. Y., Bai, S., Guo, Y., & Guo, H. (2015). A new security solution to JPEG using hyper-chaotic systems and modified zigzag scan coding. *Communications in*

Nonlinear Science and Numerical Simulation, 22(1–3), 321–333.

xviii. Wang, Y., Wong, K. W., Liao, X., & Xiang, T. (2009). A block cipher with dynamic S-boxes based on tent map. *Communications in Nonlinear Science and Numerical Simulation, 14*(7), 3089–3099.

xix. Ye, G. (2010). Image scrambling encryption algorithm of pixel bit based on chaos map. *Pattern Recognition Letters, 31*(5), 347–354.

xx. Franc, M., Grosges, T., Barchiesi, D., & Erra, R. (2012). A new image encryption scheme based on a chaotic function. *Signal Processing: Image Communication, 27*, 249–259.

xxi. Eyebe Fouda, J. S. A., Effa, J. Y., Sabat, S. L., & Ali, M. (2014). A fast chaotic block cipher for image encryption. *Communications in Nonlinear Science and Numerical Simulation, 19*(3), 578–588.

xxii. François, M., Grosges, T., Barchiesi, D., & Erra, R. (2014). Pseudo-random number generator based on mixing of three chaotic maps. *Communications in Nonlinear Science and Numerical Simulation, 19*, 887–895.

xxiii. Dastgheib, M. A., & Farhang, M. (2017). A digital pseudo-random number generator based on sawtooth chaotic map with a guaranteed enhanced period. *Nonlinear Dynamics, 89*(4), 2957–2966.

xxiv. Tong, X. J. (2012). The novel bilateral-diffusion image encryption algorithm with dynamical compound chaos. *Journal of Systems and Software, 85*(4), 850–858.

xxv. Liu, H., & Wang, X. (2013). Triple-image encryption scheme based on one-time key stream generated by chaos and plain images. *Journal of Systems and Software, 86*(3), 826–834.

xxvi. Wang, Y., Wong, K. W., Liao, X., & Chen, G. (2011). A new chaos-based fast image encryption algorithm. *Applied Soft Computing Journal, 11*(1), 514–522.

xxvii. Tong, X.-J. (2013). Design of an image encryption scheme based on a multiple chaotic map. *Communications in Nonlinear Science and Numerical Simulation, 18*(7), 1725–1733.

xxviii. Norouzi, B., Mirzakuchaki, S., Seyedzadeh, S. M., & Mosavi, M. R. (2014). A simple, sensitive and secure image encryption algorithm based on hyper-chaotic system with only one round diffusion process. *Multimedia Tools and Applications, 71*(3), 1469–1497.

xxix. Hsiao, H. I., & Lee, J. (2015). Fingerprint image cryptography based on multiple chaotic systems. *Signal Processing, 113*, 169–181.

xxx. Bhatnagar, G., & Wu, Q. M. J. (2014). Enhancing the transmission security of biometric images using chaotic encryption. *Journal of Communications and Networks, 16*(3), 203–214.

xxxi. Fu, C., Wang, X., Zhang, Y., & Chen, Y. (2013). An efficient and secure medical image protection scheme based on chaotic maps. *Computer Methods and Programs in Biomedicine, 43*(8), 1000–1010.

xxxii. Kanso, A., & Ghebleh, M. (2015). An efficient and robust image encryption scheme for medical applications. *Communications in Nonlinear Science and Numerical Simulation, 24*(1–3), 98–116.

xxxiii. Ahmad, M., & Farooq, O. (2011). Secure satellite images transmission scheme based on chaos and discrete wavelet transform. *Communications in Computer and Information Science, 169*(CCIS), 257–264.

xxxiv. Muhaya, F. T. B. (2013). Chaotic and AES cryptosystem for satellite imagery. *Telecommunication Systems, 52*(2), 573–581.

xxxv. Baptista, M. S. (1998). Cryptography with chaos. *Physics Letters A, 9601*(98), 98–101.

xxxvi. Stehelin, D., Varmus, H. E., Bishop, J. M., & Vogt, P. K. (1976). DNA related to the transforming gene(s) of avian sarcoma viruses is present in normal avian DNA. *Nature, 260*(5547), 170–173.

xxxvii. Khanzadi, H., & Eshghi, M. (2014). Image encryption using random bit sequence based on chaotic systems. *Journal of Communications, 9*(12), 1039–1047.

xxxviii. Vazquez-Medina, R., Del-Río-Correa, J. L., Rojas-López, C. E., Díaz-Méndez, J. A., Nacional, I. P., & Ana, S. (n.d.). *Image encryption without scaling and discretization process.* (No. Lcm), 105–115.

xxxix. Zhou, G., Zhang, D., Liu, Y., Yuan, Y., & Liu, Q. (2015). A novel image encryption algorithm based on chaos and line map. *Neurocomputing, 169*, 150–157.

xl. Kadir, A., Hamdulla, A., & Guo, W. Q. (2014). Color image encryption using skew tent map and hyper chaotic system of 6th-order CNN. *Optik, 125*(5), 1671–1675.

xli. Zhou, Y., Bao, L., & Chen, C. L. P. (2014). A new 1D chaotic system for image encryption. *Signal Processing, 97*(3), 172–182.

xlii. Liu, H., & Wang, X. (2010). Color image encryption based on one-time keys and robust chaotic maps. *Computers & Mathematics with Applications, 59*(10), 3320–3327.

xliii. Ye, R. (2011). An image encryption scheme with efficient permutation and diffusion processes. *Communications in Computer and Information Science, 202*(CCIS, Part 2), 32–39.

xliv. Ye, R. (2011). A novel chaos-based image encryption scheme with an efficient permutation-diffusion mechanism. *Optics Communications, 284*(22), 5290–5298.

xlv. Sui, L., Duan, K., & Liang, J. (2015). Double-image encryption based on discrete multiple-parameter fractional angular transform and two-coupled logistic maps. *Optics Communications, 343*, 140–149.

xlvi. Wang, X., Zhao, J., & Liu, H. (2012). A new image encryption algorithm based on chaos. *Optics Communications, 285*(5), 562–566.

xlvii. Eslami, Z., & Bakhshandeh, A. (2013). An improvement over an image encryption method based on total shuffling. *Optics Communications, 286*(1), 51–55.

xlviii. Jin-Mei, L., Shui-Sheng, Q., Fei, X., & Hui-Juan, X. (2008). A cryptosystem based on multiple chaotic maps. *Proceedings of the International Symposium on Information Processing (ISIP 2008)*, 740–743.

xlix. Usama, M., Khan, M. K., Alghathbar, K., & Lee, C. (2010). Chaos-based secure satellite imagery cryptosystem. *Computers & Mathematics with Applications, 60*(2), 326–337.

l. Tsekeridou, S., Solachidis, V., Nikolaidis, N., Nikolaidis, A., Tefas, A., & Pitas, I. (2001). Statistical analysis of a watermarking system based on Bernoulli chaotic sequences. *Signal Processing, 81*, 1273–1293.

li. Etemadi, S., & Mohammad, B. (2013). Chaotic image encryption system using phase-magnitude. *Proceedings of the 2013 IEEE International Conference on Cyber Technology in Automation, Control, and Intelligent Systems*, 525–537.

lii. Kumar, A., & Ghose, M. K. (2011). Extended substitution–diffusion based image cipher using chaotic standard map. *Communications in Nonlinear Science and Numerical Simulation, 16*(1), 372–382.

liii. Faragallah, O. S. (2014). Efficient confusion-diffusion chaotic image cryptosystem using enhanced standard map. *Signal, Image and Video Processing, 9*(8), 1917–1926.

liv. Patidar, V., Pareek, N. K., & Sud, K. K. (2009). A new substitution–diffusion based image cipher using chaotic standard and logistic maps. *Communications in Nonlinear Science and Numerical Simulation, 14*(7), 3056–3075.

lv. Seyedzadeh, S. M., Norouzi, B., Mosavi, M. R., & Mirzakuchaki, S. (2015). A novel color image encryption algorithm based on spatial permutation and quantum chaotic map. *Nonlinear Dynamics, 81*(1–2), 511–529.

lvi. Zhang, Q., Liu, L., & Wei, X. (2014). Improved algorithm for image encryption based on DNA encoding and multi-chaotic maps. *International Journal of Electronics and Communications (AEÜ), 68*, 186–192.

lvii. Zhu, H., Zhao, C., Zhang, X., & Yang, L. (2014). An image encryption scheme using generalized Arnold map and affine cipher. *Optik, 125*(22), 6672–6677.

lviii. Zhang, W., Wong, K., Yu, H., & Zhu, Z. (2013). An image encryption scheme using reverse 2-dimensional chaotic map and dependent diffusion. *Communications in Nonlinear Science and Numerical Simulation, 18*(8), 2066–2080.

lix. Zheng, Y., & Jin, J. (2015). A novel image encryption scheme based on Hénon map and compound spatiotemporal chaos. *Multimedia Tools and Applications, 74*(18), 7803–7820.

lx. Tong, X. J., Wang, Z., Zhang, M., Liu, Y., Xu, H., & Ma, J. (2015). An image encryption algorithm based on the perturbed high-dimensional chaotic map. *Nonlinear Dynamics, 80*(3), 1493–1508.

lxi. Liu, Z., Li, S., Liu, W., & Liu, S. (2013). Opto-digital image encryption by using Baker mapping and 1-D fractional Fourier transform. *Optics and Lasers in Engineering, 51*(3), 224–229.

lxii. Naeem, E. A., et al. (2014). Efficient implementation of chaotic image encryption in transform domains. *Journal of Systems and Software, 97*, 118–127.

lxiii. Tong, X., Wang, Z., Zhang, M., & Liu, Y. (2013). A new algorithm of the combination of image compression and encryption technology based on cross chaotic map. *Nonlinear Dynamics*, 72(1–2), 229–241.

lxiv. Tong, X., Liu, Y., Zhang, M., & Shi, H. (2012). New chaotic image encryption algorithm based on cross-mapping. *Wuhan University Journal of Natural Sciences, 17*(6), 461–467.

lxv. Mondal, B., Behera, P. K., & Gangopadhyay, S. (2020). A secure image encryption scheme based on a novel 2D sine–cosine cross-chaotic (SC3) map. *Journal of Real-Time Image Processing*, 1–15.

lxvi. Zhang, L. Y., Li, C., Wong, K. W., Shu, S., & Chen, G. (2012). Cryptanalyzing a chaos-based image encryption algorithm using alternate structure. *Journal of Systems and Software, 85*(9), 2077–2085.

lxvii. Choi, M. J., Yoon, E. J., Hong, J. W., Yoon, S. Y., & Park, D. I. (2011). Cryptanalysis of an enhanced spatiotemporal chaotic image/video cryptosystem. *EURASIP Journal on Advances in Signal Processing, 2011*, 1–10.

lxviii. Fu, C., Zhang, G. Y., Bian, O., Lei, W. M., & Hong-feng, M. (2014). A novel medical image protection scheme using a 3-dimensional chaotic system. *PLOS ONE, 9*(12), e115773.

lxix. Wu, J., Liao, X., & Yang, B. (2017). Color image encryption based on chaotic systems and elliptic curve ElGamal scheme. *Signal Processing, 141*, 109–124.

lxx. Hu, H., Liu, L., & Ding, N. (2013). Pseudorandom sequence generator based on the Chen chaotic system. *Computers in Physics Communications, 184*(3), 765–768.

lxxi. Chen, J. X., Zhu, Z. L., Fu, C., & Yu, H. (2015). Optical image encryption scheme using 3-D chaotic map based joint image scrambling and random encoding in gyrator domains. *Optics Communications, 341*, 263–270.

lxxii. Chen, J., Zhu, Z., Fu, C., Yu, H., & Zhang, L. (2015). A fast chaos-based image encryption scheme with a dynamic state variables selection mechanism. *Communications in Nonlinear Science and Numerical Simulation, 20*(3), 846–860.

lxxiii. Smaoui, N., Karouma, A., & Zribi, M. (2011). Secure communications based on the synchronization of the hyperchaotic Chen and the unified chaotic systems. *Communications in Nonlinear Science and Numerical Simulation, 16*(8), 3279–3293.

lxxiv. Salah, M., Tanougast, C., Sadoudi, S., & Bouridane, A. (2013). Synchronized hybrid chaotic generators: Application to real-time wireless speech encryption. *Communications in Nonlinear Science and Numerical Simulation, 18*(8), 2035–2047.

lxxv. Kong, H. (2002). A new chaotic attractor coined ̈. *Chaos, Solitons & Fractals, 12*(3), 659–661.

lxxvi. Liu, H., Wang, X., & Kadir, A. (2013). Color image encryption using Choquet fuzzy integral and hyper chaotic system. *Optics and Lasers in Engineering, 124*(18), 3527–3533.

lxxvii. Abundiz-Pérez, F., Cruz-Hernández, C., Murillo-Escobar, M. A., López-Gutiérrez, R. M., & Arellano-Delgado, A. (2016). A fingerprint image encryption scheme based on hyperchaotic Rössler map. *Mathematical Problems in Engineering, 2016*, 1–15.

lxxviii. Kanso, A., & Ghebleh, M. (2012). A novel image encryption algorithm based on a 3D chaotic map. *Communications in Nonlinear Science and Numerical Simulation, 17*(7), 2943–2959.

lxxix. Liu, H., Wang, X., & Kadir, A. (2013). Color image encryption using Choquet fuzzy integral and hyper chaotic system. *Optik (Stuttgart), 124*(18), 3527–3533.

lxxx. Guesmi, R., & Ben Farah, M. A. (2020). A new efficient medical image cipher based on hybrid chaotic map and DNA code. *Journal of Applied Sciences, 20*, 1–15.

lxxxi. Liu, Y., & Zhang, J. (2020). A multidimensional chaotic image encryption algorithm based on DNA coding. *Multimedia Tools and Applications, 79*(29–30), 21579–21601.

lxxxii. Kumar, M., Powduri, P., & Reddy, A. (2014). An RGB image encryption using diffusion process associated with chaotic map. *ScienceDirect*, 1–15.

lxxxiii. Patro, K. A. K., & Acharya, B. (2020). A novel multi-dimensional multiple image encryption technique. *Multimedia Tools and Applications*, 79(19–20), 12959–12994.

CHAPTER 3
Pseudo-Random Number Generation Based on Fusional Chaotic Maps

3.1. Introduction

The requirement of randomness has gained interest in the field of random number generation, specifically in the use of these random numbers for secure digital data transmission. They also play a vital role in different industries, such as simulations, gambling, one-time password generation in money transfer applications, and particularly in cryptography for generating unpredictable key series [1]. Random numbers have been generated by two modes: True Random Number Generator (TRNG) and Pseudo-Random Number Generator (PRNG). TRNGs are generated by some physical resources and are non-deterministic, which makes them insufficient for key generation in cryptosystems. The random number generator PRNG is deterministic and also has good randomness. These qualities make it suitable for utilization in key generation for cryptosystems [2]. Some of the common PRNGs utilized in cryptosystems include the Linear Congruential Generator (LCG) [3], Elliptic Curve [4], Linear Feedback Shift Register (LFSR) [5], and non-linear chaos-based PRNGs [6], [7]. Among these methods, chaos-based random number generation has become popular among cryptographers because of its inherent properties, such as ergodicity, high randomness, and sensitivity to initial parameters. Specifically, chaotic systems generate deterministic numbers with good randomness, which is the most important aspect of key generation in cryptosystems [8].

Chaotic maps are categorized into lower- and higher-dimensional chaotic systems, depending on the number of key series generated by the chaotic map [9]–[11]. Many chaos-based cryptosystems [12]–[16] have been developed by combining different lower-dimensional maps. Patidar et al. advanced a new confusion and diffusion process to encrypt images by utilizing two lower-depth chaotic maps, namely the 1D logistic map and the 2D standard map [17]. Fu et al. [18] proposed a cryptosystem by blending the Arnold cat map and the 1D logistic map, which is specifically used for medical images. Fewer rounds of confusion and diffusion are executed for encryption to provide reliable security for medical images. Most low-dimensional chaos-based image cryptosystems have achieved satisfactory results. However, as Zheng et al. [19] specified, low-dimensional chaotic systems have two main drawbacks—limited random periods of chaotic series and lower key space—which are insufficient to resist different attacks. Many lower-dimensional chaos image cryptosystems have been cryptanalyzed [20]–[22].

Hence, to overcome these drawbacks, different researchers have designed various fusional 2D chaotic maps with efficient key space and long-term random behavior. A few newly designed fusional 2D chaotic maps are discussed in the succeeding section.

3.2. Existing Fusional Chaotic Maps

Zhou et al. [23] introduced a new Parametric Switching Chaotic System (PSCS) by combining three existing maps to efficiently encrypt images. Pixel positions of the image are permuted using the 2D PSCS transform, and substitution is carried out using the 1D PSCS to produce encrypted templates. Liao et al. [24] developed a new 2D Henon-Sine Map (2D HSM), which generates good pseudo-random chaotic series. The chaotic behavior of these series has been proved by executing trajectories of chaotic series and Lyapunov exponent values. Further, these chaotic series have been utilized for developing an efficient image cryptosystem.

A new 2D Chebyshev-Sine Map was designed by Liu et al. [25], which produces a better pseudo-random sequence than the seed maps such as the 1D Chebyshev and Sine maps. The generated chaotic sequences are utilized for efficiently encrypting color images. Behera et al. [26] designed a new 2D Sine-Cosine-Cross-Chaotic (SC3) map by combining the 1D Sine and 2D Cross chaotic maps. The evaluation of sensitivity to initial conditions has been identified by calculating the Lyapunov exponent of the 2D SC3 map. This map generates two pseudo-random sequences, R1 and R2, which are utilized in developing an image cryptosystem. Many researchers have developed different 2D chaotic PRNGs by combining existing 1D and 2D chaotic systems, achieving efficient randomness [27]–[29].

3.3. Proposed Fusional Chaotic Map

Inspired by the above fusional 2D chaotic maps, a new fusional 2D chaotic map has been proposed by combining two chaotic maps with efficient random behavior. A new 2D Cross Cosine Map (CCM) is proposed by combining the 1D Chebyshev map and the 2D Cross chaotic map. Its dynamical form is analyzed and verified to be chaotic. Initial and system parameters are increased, and their ranges are also expanded. Hence, the key space is enhanced, making it sufficient for adoption in cryptosystems. The following subsections deal with the representation of the novel fusional chaotic map.

3.3.1. Chebyshev Map

Chebyshev map, a well-known 1D non-linear map [30], is expressed in Equation (3.1). It has both chaotic and semigroup properties and good ergodicity. The chaotic series generated by the map has a uniform distribution.

$$x_{n+1} = cos(\lambda \, cos^{-1}(x_n)) \quad (3.1)$$

where $x_n \in [-1, 1]$, x_0 is the initial parameter, and λ is the system parameter. The map generates chaotic series in a chaotic state when $\lambda \in [2, \infty)$

3.3.2. Cross-Chaotic Map

The cross-chaotic map is introduced by Tong et al. [31]. It has been proved that 2D cross-chaotic map has a high degree of randomness compared to traditional 2D Logistic maps. Its mathematical form is expressed in Equation. (3.2).

$$\begin{aligned} x_i &= sin^2(3 \, arcsin\sqrt{|y_{i-1}|}) \\ y_i &= 4x_{i-1}^3 - 3x_{i-1} \end{aligned} \quad (3.2)$$

where x_0 and $y_0 \in (0, 1)$ are the initial parameters

Despite the high degree of randomness of the cross-chaotic map, only two initial parameters can be reserved as keys. This key size is insufficient to create an optimal cryptosystem. In order to resolve this problem, a new fusion chaotic map with sufficient key size is proposed.

3.3.3. Fusional 2D CCM

It is well known that the key size is a significant metric to measure the strength of the cryptosystem. For chaos based cryptosystems, the initial and system parameters values of chaotic map are considered as keys. Even, the above-discussed maps have sufficient random chaotic series, but they are lack in key size and simple structure, which makes their orbits can be easily predicted by chaotic signal estimation technologies [32]. To address this issue, a new 2D CCM is proposed with an enhanced key size from 10^{28} to 10^{56} to strengthen the cryptosystem. Performance validation indicates, that the 2D-CCM has better ergodicity, wider chaotic range and unpredictability than the seed chaotic maps. The proposed 2D CCM is expressed in Equation (3.3).

$$\left.\begin{aligned} x_i &= sin^2\left(\alpha sin^{-1}(\sqrt{|y_{i-1}|})\right) & \alpha, \alpha > 1 \\ y_i &= cos^2\left(\beta cos^{-1}(\sqrt{|x_{i-1}|})\right) & \beta, \beta > 1 \end{aligned}\right\} - \left(\begin{matrix} System \\ Parameters \end{matrix}\right) \quad (3.3)$$

where x_0, $y_0 \in (0, 1)$ are the initial parameters, and the system parameters α, β should be in intervals as stated above in order to produce random chaotic key series.

3.4. *Performance Analysis*

This section evaluates the efficiency and randomness of 2D CCM function based on spatiotemporal analysis, lyapunov exponent, bifurcation diagram, key space analysis, and finally the randomness is assessed by statistical NIST test suite.

3.4.1. Chaotic Behaviour Analysis

In order to prove the chaotic property, 2D CCM is executed iteratively for 5000 times with key values x_0 = 0.35678556782346, y_0 = 0.53456765786432, α = 1234567891011 and β = 110987654321. Figure 3.1 illustrates the correlation analysis of X and Y chaotic series and proves that the proposed 2D CCM has optimal random behaviour and statistical properties.

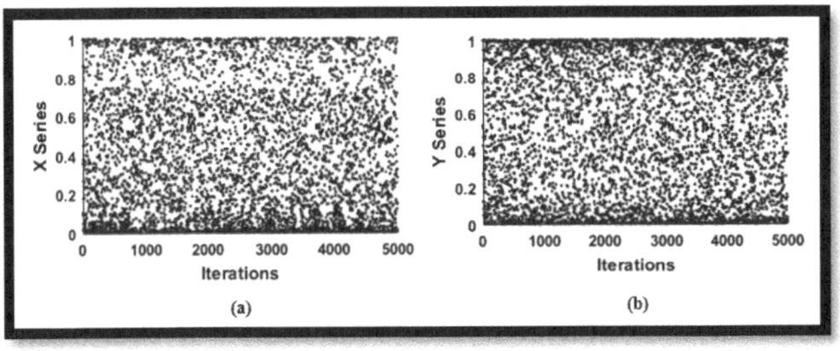

Figure 3.1 Spatiotemporal Diagram of 2D CCM System A) X Series B) Y Series

3.4.2. Lyapunov Exponent and Bifurcation Analysis

Lyapunov Exponent (LE) λ is the most common method to measure the degree of chaos [33]. It is used to find how chaotic behaviour changes with varying system parameters. The orbit of the chaotic map is said to be chaotic only when $\lambda > 0$. Figure 3.2 (a) shows the LE spectrum of the proposed 2D CCM, where the range of system parameter $\alpha \in (1,10]$ with has an increment of $\Delta\alpha = 0.01$. From Figure 3.2 (a), it can be identified that λ value is always positive for the parameter $\alpha \geq 2$. This proves the dynamic state of the proposed map. The bifurcation diagram in Figure. 3.2 (b) demonstrates that the 2D CCM has a complex set of periodic orbits and trajectories. Figure.3.2 (c) indicates the trajectories of X and Y chaotic series, representing no correlation among X and Y chaotic series even though they are dependent on each other.

3.4.3. Key Space Analysis

Key space analysis is one of the most important analyses that must be performed to evaluate the performance and security of chaotic maps in order to check whether they are suitable for information security applications. Key space, in general, reflects the system's resistance to brute-force attacks. Even if the seed map has a sufficiently random chaotic series, it lacks key size and also has a simple structure, which makes its orbits easily predictable by chaotic signal estimation technologies [32].

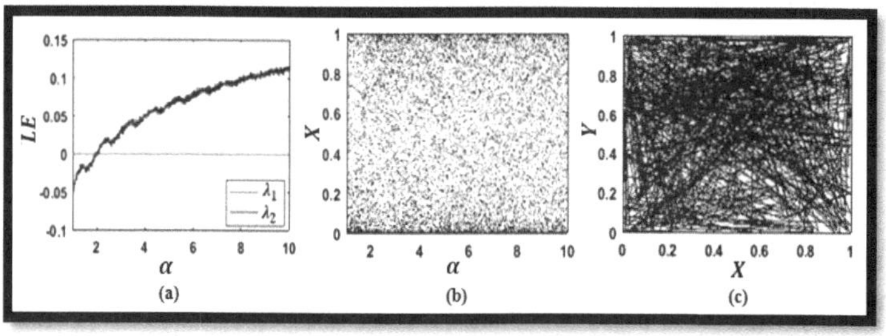

Figure 3.2: Chaotic Behaviour Analysis of 2D CCM A) Lyapunov Exponent B) Bifurcation Diagram C) Trajectories of X and Y

To address this issue, the proposed 2D CCM has four secret keys $\{x_0, y_0, \alpha, \beta\}$ and the size of each key can reach the maximum value of $\alpha \times \beta \times 10^{28}$ and x_0, y_0 for the precision value of 10^{-14} , then the total key size is enhanced to 10^{56} which is higher than the seed map having the key size as 10^{28}. Hence, the key size of the proposed 2D CCM is $((10^{56} \approx 2^{140}) > 2^{128}))$, which is very higher than the existing seed cross chaotic map $(10^{28} \approx 2^{85}) < 2^{128}$) to resist brute-force attack.

3.4.4. Statistical Analysis of the Pseudorandom Bits Generated by 2D CCM

A good chaotic sequence should have sufficient statistical properties. For determining the randomness of the 2D CCM chaotic sequence, an internationally accepted NIST statistical test suite is used. NIST suite is a collection of sixteen different statistical tests [34]. A good chaotic bit series should pass in all the test cases. 400000 pseudo-random bits are generated using the proposed 2D CCM and tested in the NIST suite. The length of the binary string for Maurer's universal statistical test has to be > = 387840 bits. Therefore, 400000 bits are taken as inputs and are tested for randomness. Table 3.1 shows that the proposed 2D CCM successfully passed in all the NIST suite test cases. This indicates that the proposed X and Y chaotic series has sufficient randomness and can adapt to develop image cryptosystem.

NIST Statistical Tests	Probability-Value of (X)	Probability-Value of (Y)	Result
Frequency test -monobit	0.05029	0.47287	Pass
Cumulative sums (Forward)	0.05012	0.49574	Pass
Cumulative sums (Reverse)	0.05012	0.49574	Pass
Block frequency test	0.15702	0.27308	Pass
Runs test	0.20121	0.65053	Pass
Binary matrix rank test	0.80715	0.25492	Pass
Longest run test	0.38287	0.70313	Pass
Overlapping templates test	0.33010	0.38353	Pass
Discrete Fourier transform test	0.32381	0.18191	Pass
Approximate entropy	0.63147	0.90980	Pass

test			
Maurer's universal statistical test	0.56871	0.09349	Pass
Random excursions variant test	0.71307	0.86220	Pass
Random excursions test	0.12874	0.82767	Pass
Linear complexity test	0.88068	0.67258	Pass
Serial test 1	0.67147	0.83416	Pass
Serial test 2	0.08104	0.83021	Pass

Table 3.1: NIST Test Suite Results of 2D CCM

3.5. Chapter Summary

An efficient and secure PRNG has been proposed for generating pseudo-random numbers. The developed fusional map has achieved an enhanced key space of 10^{58} and is also highly sensitive to initial and system parameters. The chaotic series of 2D CCM has been successfully approved by the statistical NIST suite, passing all the test cases. This map is useful for achieving better results with reduced computational cost compared to other higher-dimensional chaotic maps in the upcoming chapters.

3.6. References

i. Hill, D. R. C. (2003). URNG: A portable optimization technique for software applications requiring pseudo-random numbers. *Simulation Modelling Practice and Theory, 11*(7–8), 643–654.

ii. Behnia, S., Akhavan, A., Akhshani, A., & Samsudin, A. (2011). A novel dynamic model of pseudo-random number generator. *Journal of Computational and Applied Mathematics, 235*(12), 3455-3463.

iii. Meidl, W., & Winterhof, A. (2007). On the linear complexity profile of nonlinear congruential pseudorandom number generators with Rédei functions. *Finite Fields and Their Applications, 13*(3), 628–634.

iv. Chervyakov, N. I., Babenko, M. G., Kucherov, N. N., Kuchukov, V. A., & Shabalina, M. N. (2016). Researches of algorithm of PRNG on the basis of bilinear pairing on points of an elliptic curve with use of a neural network. *Advances in Intelligent Systems and Computing, 427*, 167–173.

v. Marchi, A., Liverani, A., & Del Giudice, A. (2009). Polynomial pseudo-random number generator via cyclic phase. *Mathematics and Computers in Simulation, 79*(11), 3328–3338.

vi. Han, C., Wang, Y., Liu, Y., & Li, D. (2013). Two improved pseudo-random number generation algorithms based on the logistic map. *Nonlinear Science Letters A, 5*(6), 2174–2179.

vii. Elsherbeny, M. N., & Rahal, M. (2012). Pseudo-random number generator using deterministic chaotic system. *International Journal of Scientific & Technology Research, 1*(9), 95–97.

viii. Dastgheib, M. A., & Farhang, M. (2017). A digital pseudo-random number generator based on sawtooth chaotic map with a guaranteed enhanced period. *Nonlinear Dynamics, 89*(4), 2957–2966.

ix. Seyedzadeh, S. M., Norouzi, B., Mosavi, M. R., & Mirzakuchaki, S. (2015). A novel color image encryption algorithm based on spatial permutation and quantum chaotic map. *Nonlinear Dynamics, 81*(1–2), 511–529.

x. Ye, R. (2011). A novel chaos-based image encryption scheme with an efficient permutation-diffusion mechanism. *Optical Communications, 284*(22), 5290–5298.

xi. Faragallah, O. S. (2014). Efficient confusion-diffusion chaotic image cryptosystem using enhanced standard map. *Signal, Image, and Video Processing, 9*(8), 1917–1926.

xii. Anees, A. (2015). An image encryption scheme based on Lorenz system for low profile applications. *3D Research, 6*(3), 1–10.

xiii. Huang, X., & Ye, G. (2012). An image encryption algorithm based on hyper-chaos and DNA sequence.

xiv. Hu, T., Liu, Y., Gong, L.-H., & Ouyang, C.-J. (2016). An image encryption scheme combining chaos with cycle operation for DNA sequences. *Nonlinear Dynamics.*

xv. Khan, M., & Shah, T. (2014). A novel image encryption technique based on Hènon chaotic map and S8 symmetric group. *Neural Computing and Applications, 25*(7), 1717–1722.

xvi. Zhang, X., Fan, X., Wang, J., & Zhao, Z. (2016). A chaos-based image encryption scheme using 2D rectangular transform and dependent substitution. *Multimedia Tools and Applications, 75*(4), 1745–1763.

xvii. Patidar, V., Pareek, N. K., & Sud, K. K. (2009). A new substitution-diffusion based image cipher using chaotic standard and logistic maps. *Communications in Nonlinear Science and Numerical Simulation, 14*(7), 3056–3075.

xviii. Fu, C., et al. (2013). An efficient and secure medical image protection scheme based on chaotic maps. *Computers in Biology and Medicine, 43*(8), 1000–1010.

xix. Zheng, Y., & Jin, J. (2015). A novel image encryption scheme based on Hénon map and compound spatiotemporal chaos. *Multimedia Tools and Applications, 74*(18), 7803–7820.

xx. Choi, M. J., Yoon, E. J., Hong, J. W., Yoon, S. Y., & Park, D. I. (2011). Cryptanalysis of an enhanced spatiotemporal chaotic image/video cryptosystem. *EURASIP Journal on Advances in Signal Processing.*

xxi. Rhouma, R., & Belghith, S. (2011). Cryptanalysis of a chaos-based cryptosystem on DSP. *Communications in Nonlinear Science and Numerical Simulation, 16*(2), 876–884.

xxii. Bechikh, R., Hermassi, H., El-latif, A. A. A., Rhouma, R., & Belghith, S. (2015). Breaking an image encryption scheme based on a spatiotemporal chaotic system. *Signal Processing: Image Communication, 39*, 151–158.

xxiii. Zhou, Y., Bao, L., & Chen, C. L. P. (2013). Image encryption using a new parametric switching chaotic system. *Signal Processing, 93*(11), 3039–3052.

xxiv. Wu, J., Liao, X., & Yang, B. (2018). Image encryption using 2D Hénon-Sine map and DNA approach. *Signal Processing, 153*, 11–23.

xxv. Liu, H. (2018). Construction of a new 2D Chebyshev-Sine map and its application to color image encryption. *Multimedia Tools and Applications.*

xxvi. Mondal, B., Behera, P. K., & Gangopadhyay, S. (2020). A secure image encryption scheme based on a novel 2D sine–cosine cross-chaotic (SC3) map. *Journal of Real-Time Image Processing.*

xxvii. Liu, W., Sun, K., & He, S. (2017). SF-SIMM high-dimensional hyperchaotic map and its performance analysis. *Nonlinear Dynamics, 89*(4), 2521–2532.

xxviii. Zhang, Y., & Xiao, D. (2013). Double optical image encryption using discrete Chirikov standard map and chaos-based fractional random transform. *Optics and Lasers in Engineering, 51*(4), 472–480.

xxix. Mondal, B., Kumar, P., & Singh, S. (2018). A chaotic permutation and diffusion based image encryption algorithm for secure communications. *Multimedia Tools and Applications, 77*(23), 31177–31198.

xxx. Attaullah, A., Javeed, A., & Shah, T. (2019). Cryptosystem techniques based on the improved Chebyshev map: an application in image encryption. *Multimedia Tools and Applications, 78*(22), 31467–31484.

xxxi. Tong, X., Liu, Y., Zhang, M., & Shi, H. (2012). New chaotic image encryption algorithm based on cross-mapping. *Wuhan University Journal of Natural Sciences, 17*(6), 461–467.

xxxii. Liu, H., Wen, F., & Kadir, A. (2019). Construction of a new 2D Chebyshev-Sine map and its application to color image encryption. *Multimedia Tools and Applications, 78*(12), 15997–16010.

xxxiii. Ali, T. S., & Ali, R. (2020). A new chaos based color image encryption algorithm using permutation substitution and Boolean operation. *Multimedia Tools and Applications, 79*(27–28), 19853–19873.

xxxiv. Xiang, H., & Liu, L. (2020). An improved digital logistic map and its application in image encryption. *Multimedia Tools and Applications.*

CHAPTER 4

A Novel Cross Cosine Map Based Medical Image Cryptosystem Using Dynamic Bit-Level Diffusion

4.1. Introduction

With the breakneck pace of development in medical technology, the transmission of medical information related to diagnosis, surgery, and telemedicine via insecure networks has become an absolute necessity. In such circumstances, there arises an exigent need to protect the confidentiality of patients' data [1]. In the present times, techniques like Magnetic Resonance Imaging (MRI), Positron Emission Tomography (PET), and Computed Tomography (CT) help examine the internal organs of patients for diagnostic purposes. These medical images are widely stored in Digital Imaging and Communications in Medicine (DICOM) format or Picture Archiving and Communication System (PACS) format. Among these formats, DICOM is widely used to embed patient details as an invisible and permanent watermark [2].

The widespread use of medical images has led to research related to their storage, processing, security, and transmission [3]. When it comes to security, medical images demand the highest level of integrity, confidentiality, and authenticity [4]. As per the report of HealthCare IT News released in 2019 [5], medical information is often stolen for committing insurance fraud, blackmailing, and spying. According to the IT report, the second most targeted industry for data breaches in 2019 was the medical/healthcare sector, which also ranked second in terms of exposing sensitive records. Hence, the security of medical documents has received utmost priority in the field of medical technology. Steganography and cryptography are two different mechanisms used for ensuring the security of multimedia content. In steganography, Electronic Patient Records (EPR) and other report information are embedded in medical images. Whenever doctors need the report, they extract those records from the image for diagnosis. Embedding EPR in medical images secures the patient's information [6]. However, these medical images are transmitted and stored in their original form in the network and repository, making them vulnerable to various attacks. In such a situation, encrypting medical images has been found to be an efficient technique when combined with steganography to address security and confidentiality concerns.

Conventional algorithms like AES, DES, and IDEA [7] have been applied for securing medical images. However, due to the inherent qualities of medical images, such as large data size, high pixel redundancy, and strong correlation among picture elements, traditional algorithms fail to provide optimal security [8], [9]. To overcome these limitations, various image cryptosystems have been developed over the past decades. Chaos-based cryptosystems have fascinated researchers due to characteristics like randomness, determinism, ergodicity, and high sensitivity to initial conditions [10], [11]. These features make chaos a suitable choice for image cryptosystems. Extensive research has been conducted on chaos-based image cryptosystems [12], [13]. However, studies related to chaos-based medical image cryptosystems remain limited. Some of the chaos-based medical image cryptosystems developed so far are briefly discussed in the following section.

A typical chaos-based image cipher architecture involves two processes: confusion and diffusion [14]. The following research works employ this cipher pattern. Hua et al. [15] advanced a high-speed scrambling model-based medical image cryptosystem. In this model, pixel scrambling is performed using random data generated by a logistic sine map, while two arithmetic operations—modulo and XOR—are used for pixel diffusion to produce the final cipher image. Hu et al. [16] proposed an efficient encryption method that uses multi-scroll chaos. In this method, the medical image is encrypted using row and column round scrambling, and a simple XOR operation is used for substitution. Fu et al. [17] utilized an Arnold cat map chaotic series to reduce pixel correlation in a DICOM image. Then, a chaotic series of the 1D logistic map is used to diffuse the image. Ravichandran et al. [18] developed a new Chao-cryptic system based on three different chaotic maps. In this system, medical images are permuted using a chaotic series of the logistic-tent map. Then, XOR-ing is used to diffuse the pixels with the chaotic series of a logistic sine map to obtain an encrypted image. Satheshkumar et al. [19] proposed a dual chaos-based circular shifting method in which the original image is divided into blocks and scanned in a zigzag fashion to create a permuted image. The permuted image is then diffused using a 1D logistic and Bernoulli map chaotic series.

All the medical image cryptosystems discussed above have utilized lower-dimensional chaotic maps for the confusion and diffusion processes to achieve good encryption results. However, Mondal et al. [20] remarked that a few initial seed keys can be easily estimated, and the low-complexity structure of lower-dimensional map cryptosystems makes them vulnerable to various attacks. Specifically, these cryptosystems can be cryptanalyzed using chosen/known plaintext attacks. Liu et al. [21] cryptanalyzed the 1D coupled sine map-based image cipher by executing a chosen plaintext attack. Huang et al. [22] identified the vulnerabilities of 1D chaos-based image cryptosystems [23] and proposed a collision-based technique to break the cryptosystem using a chosen ciphertext attack. Likewise, various cryptanalysts have successfully cracked multiple lower-dimensional cryptographic image architectures [24], [25]. Consequently, the state-of-the-art medical image cryptosystems discussed above may be vulnerable to known/chosen ciphertext attacks.

To address the issue of limited key space in cryptosystems, some schemes have employed higher-dimensional chaotic maps to develop cryptographic models with larger key sizes. Various researchers have developed higher-dimensional map-based medical image cryptosystems, which are discussed as follows: Chen et al. [26] utilized a Four-Dimensional (4D) Lorenz chaotic map to develop a hierarchical diffusion-based medical image cipher with a sufficiently large key size. Additionally, they diffused the pixels in a non-sequential manner, which enhanced security. Chai et al. [27] proposed a new 4D memristive chaotic system by enhancing the features of a three-dimensional four-wing system. They adopted the Latin square for medical image permutation, while the chaotic series of the 4D memristive map was used for the diffusion process, making the cryptosystem more secure than lower-dimensional maps. Stalin et al. [28] developed a fast and secure medical image architecture by proposing a novel 4D Logistic map, which has a larger key space than the 1D Logistic map. They adopted a new DNA computation technique in the diffusion phase to enhance cryptosystem security. However, while these higher-dimensional chaotic map-based medical image cryptosystems offer a large key space, they fail to achieve all the essential properties of a strong cryptosystem, such as robust diffusion, plain-image dependence, and dynamic seed key generation. They also suffer from weaknesses like structural complexity and high implementation costs.

The challenges associated with current chaos-based medical image cryptosystems have motivated the development of a new medical image cryptosystem with a large key space, sufficient randomness, and sustainable uniform key distribution over an extended period with reduced computational costs. In this context, this work proposes a 2D CCM-based medical image cryptosystem. Furthermore, to make this cryptosystem dependent on plain images, SHA-256 has been applied to generate dynamic seed keys, strengthening the cryptosystem's resilience against known and chosen plaintext attacks. These dynamic seed keys serve as the initial parameters for the proposed 2D CCM in Chapter 3, generating a more efficient random chaotic series than existing seed maps. Additionally, a new dynamic Bit-Flipping method has been introduced in the diffusion phase, specifically tailored for different modalities of medical images. For 8-bit depth X-ray images, the flip-key range for Bit-Flipping is 1 to 8, whereas, for 15-bit depth MRI and CT scan images, the flip-key range is from 1 to 16. This ensures that the cryptosystem is suitable for all medical image modalities. Moreover, the dynamic Bit-Flipping process significantly reduces pixel correlation in medical images, which typically exhibit higher redundancy and pixel correlation than regular images. Finally, the developed cryptosystem fulfills the essential properties of a robust cryptographic model, such as strong diffusion, plain-image dependence, and a dynamic key series. These attributes distinguish the proposed model from existing cryptosystems.

4.1.1. Contributions of 2D-CCM Model

The significant contributions of the proposed crypt model are précised as follows:

i. An efficient medical image cryptosystem using a 2D CCM chaotic series-based permutation and dynamic Bit-Flipping-based diffusion is proposed to secure medical images.
ii. The chaotic series generated by 2D CCM is used for random pixel-level permutation and bit-level permutation to achieve efficient confusion and diffusion.
iii. To achieve strong diffusion, a novel dynamic Bit-Flipping process is proposed, especially for medical images. In this process, each pixel's bit values are randomly flipped depending on the bit depth of the medical images. Thus, it increases the security level of the cryptosystem.
iv. Dynamic seed keys of the 2D CCM are generated based on the plain image by applying SHA-256.

Subsequently, the cryptosystem can withstand chosen/known plaintext attacks.

v. Security and performance analyses are evaluated through simulations. The outcome of the analyses is evidence that the proposed crypto model is more secure and suitable for ensuring the confidentiality and integrity of medical images during transmission and storage.

4.2.2D CCM in Medical Image Cryptosystem

A detailed discussion on the development of 2D CCM and its chaotic behavior is provided in Chapter 3.

4.2.1. Seed Key Generation of 2D-CCM Using SHA-256

In the developed cryptosystem, a 256-bit internal private key (H) has been employed. The private key is produced using SHA-256 hash function and has the potential of withstanding chosen/known-plaintext attacks [12]. The initial and parameter values of 2D CCM are updated using the secret key (H) taken from the original image. The 64-digit hexadecimal hash value is divided into eight groups, i.e., $h_{k1,}\ h_{k2,}h_{k3} \dots h_{k8,}, k = 1,2 \dots 16$. each group contains 16 hexadecimal values. The generation of seed keys using SHA-256 hash value is expressed in Equation. (4.1) below.

$$\begin{array}{ll} hx_{k1} = hex_{xor}(h_{k1}, h_{k2}) & hx_{k2} = hex_{xor}(h_{k3}, h_{k4}) \\ hx_{k3} = hex_{xor}(h_{k5}, h_{k6}) & hx_{k4} = hex_{xor}(h_{k7}, h_{k8}) \end{array} \quad (4.1)$$

Here, the eight groups of hexadecimal values are converted into four groups by executing XOR operation on each pair of groups. Execution of Hex-XOR operation is done using HEX-XOR Table [29]. From these four groups, two groups are taken for seed key generation and another two groups are used for system parameters. This is represented in Equation. (4.2) below.

$$key_1 = hex2dec(hx_{k1}) \times 10^{-16} \quad key_2 = hex2dec(hx_{k2}) \times 10^{-16}$$
$$key_3 = hex2dec(hx_{k3}) \times 10^{16} \quad key_4 = hex2dec(hx_{k4}) \times 10^{16} \qquad (4.2)$$

If $\{x_0, y_0, \alpha, \beta\}$ are considered as external seed keys and system parameters of 2D-CCM to generate chaotic series, then for each specific medical image, the new seed keys $\{x_0', y_0'\}$ and parameters $\{\alpha', \beta'\}$ are generated using Equation (4.3).

$$x_0' = (x_0 + key_1) mod\,1 \quad y_0' = (y_0 + key_2)\, mod\,1$$
$$\alpha' = \alpha \oplus key_3 \quad \beta' = \beta \oplus key_4 \qquad (4.3)$$

From equations (4.1 - 4.3), it can be found that the seed keys and parameters $\{x_0', y_0', \alpha', \beta'\}$ depends on the plain image. If there is a difference in just one bit of the plain image, the SHA-256 produces an entirely different hash value. Hence, our proposed cryptosystem is highly sensitive to the original image.

4.2.2. Encryption Process

The 2D CCM based medical image cryptosystem combines three phases, namely key generation, confusion, and diffusion. Figure 4.1 shows the block design of the developed cryptosystem. The initial external seed values are updated using SHA-256 and used as secret keys in the developed cryptosystems. The number of keys and key size are directly proportional to the security level of the cryptosystem. Here, four external keys $\{x_0, y_0, \alpha, \beta\}$ and 256 - bit hash value are taken as seed keys. These keys are fed in to 2D CCM to generate chaotic series $X = \{x_1, x_2, x_3, x_4 \ldots x_{(M \times N)/2}\}$ and $Y = \{y_1, y_2, y_3, y_4 \ldots y_{(M \times N)/2}\}$ and used to accomplish the confusion process. The diffusion process is executed using Bit-Flipping and XOR operations. The systematic execution of encryption and decryption is discussed in the following section. Confusion and diffusion process are executed, as shown in Algorithms 1 and 2.

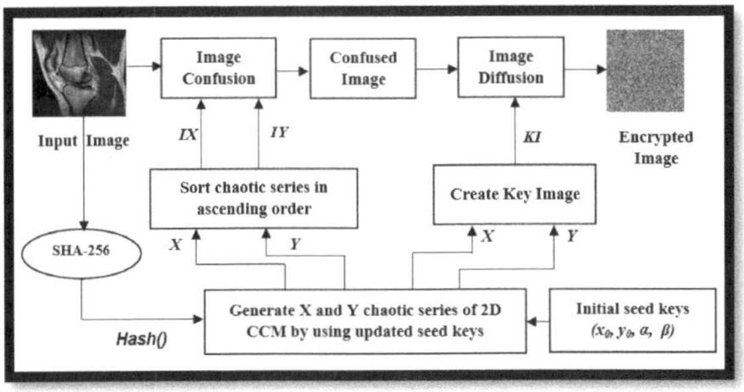

Figure 4.1: Architecture of 2D CCM Based Medical Image Cryptosystem

Step 1: Input image I(M × N), (8-bit or 16-bit) where M and N denote number of rows (Height) and columns (Width) of the respective input image.

Step 2: Create pair of chaotic sequences $X = \{x_1, x_2, x_3, x_4 \ldots x_{(M \times N)/2}\}$ and $Y = \{y_1, y_2, y_3, y_4 \ldots y_{(M \times N)/2}\}$ using the proposed 2D CCM and by taking $\{x'_0, y'_0, \alpha', \beta'\}$ as secret keys.

Step 3: Sort the two chaotic streams X and Y to obtain the index value used for the confusion process. The sorting logic is expressed in Equation (4.4) .

$[SOX, IOX] = sort(X);\ [SOY, IOY] = sort(Y)$ (4.4)

Where, SOX, SOY are the sorted sequence of X, Y and IOX, IOY are the index values of SOX, SOY.

Step 4: In confusion process, pixel positions of Image (I) are scrambled using index values (IOX and IOY) as expressed in Equation (4.5).

$I'_{i,j} <=> I_{IOX(i),IOY(i)}$ *Where,* $i = j = 1, 2, 3 \ldots M/N$ (4.5)

When all the pixel positions are scrambled, then the result will be the confused image I' .Figure 4.2 illustrates the process of confusion by taking 10 pixels of the image and shows the output of the confused image.

Step 5: Generate Key Image (KI) by combining X and Y chaotic series. Equation (4.6) below illustrates the creation of KI. In the equation, MaxPixel specifies the image's maximum pixel value; 255 is the largest intensity of the 8-bit image.

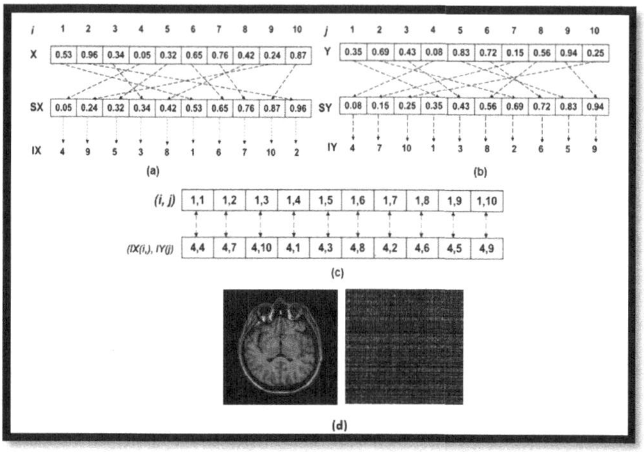

Figure 4.2 : Illustration of the confusion process a) i, IX series denote the row of the image b) j, IY series denote the columns of the Image c) Illustration of row permutation with 10 Pixels d) Original image and their corresponding confused image

$$\begin{cases} KI(i,j) = mod((X(p) \times 10^{14}), MaxPixel)) \; if(mod(j,2) == 0) \\ KI(i,j) = mod((Y(q) \times 10^{14}), MaxPixel)) \; if(mod(j,2) \neq 0) \end{cases} \quad (4.6)$$

$$Where, \begin{cases} i,j = 1,2,3 \ldots M/\,N \\ p,q = 1,2,3,\ldots (M \times N)/2 \end{cases}$$

The KI should be created based on the size of the original image, odd columns of KI is filled with Y chaotic series, and even columns are filled with X chaotic series, and these chaotic series are converted into integer form using mod operation.

Step 6: Convert the confused image to binary form and flip the binary value of each pixel based on their parallel KI values as expressed in Equation (4.7).

$$BI(i,j) = Convert\ To\ Binary\big(I'(i,j)\big)$$
$$flipbits = 8 - mod(KI(i,j), 7) \qquad Where, i, j$$
$$FI(i,j) = flipud(BI(i,j), flipbits)$$
$$= 1,2,3, \ldots \frac{M}{N} \quad (4.7)$$

Figure 4.3 below shows the Bits-Flipping process of an 8-bit image in detail, wherein values 8 and 7 are used to find the number of bits that have to be flipped. In the medical field, X-ray and ultrasound grayscale images are represented in 8-bit depth, So for this type of images, the flipbits range from 1 to 8. Further, CT and MRI scan images are represented in 16-bit depth, so the flipbits range will be 1-16, to obtain this range instead of 8 and 7, 16 and 15 should be used for identifying the flipbits in Equation (4.7).

Step 7: Obtain the final cipher image CI from the binary flipped image FI by performing XOR operation as expressed in Equation (4.8) below.

$$CI(row, col) =$$
$$\begin{cases} FI(1,1) \oplus KI(1,1)\ row = col = 2,3, \ldots \ldots \frac{M}{N} \\ FI(row, col) \oplus previous\big(CI(row, col)\big) \oplus KI(row, col) \end{cases}$$

(4.8)

The final cipher image CI has a noisy structure.

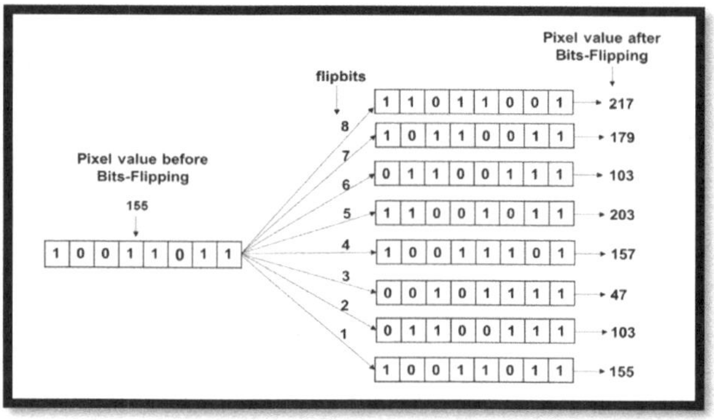

Figure 4.3: Demonstration of Bits-Flipping using a Single 8-Bit Pixel Value for All Possible Flip Bits

***Algorithm 1:* Confusion process of the proposed medical image encryption**

Input: *I = read Image ('Input image')* **Keys** :$\{x'_0, y'_0, \alpha', \beta'\}$

Output: *I' (Confused Image)*

1. *[M, N] = size of (I)*
2. *X =zeros((M×N)/2)), Y=zeros(((M×N)/2))*
3. *[X, Y] = 2D-CCM* $(x'_0, y'_0, \alpha', \beta')$
4. *[SOX,IOX] = sort(X); [SOY,IOY] =sort(Y)*
5. **For** *row=1 to M* **do**
6. **For** *col=1 to N* **do**
7. *I'(row, col) = swap(I(row, col), I(IX(row) , IY(col)))*
8. ***End***
9. ***End***

***Algorithm 2:* Diffusion Process of proposed medical image encryption**

Input: *I' (Confused image)* ***Keys*** *: X,Y*

Ouptut: *CI(Cipher Image)*

1. $p = q = (M \times N)/2$

2\. **For** *I =1 to M* **Do**
3\. **For** *j=1 to N* **Do**
4\. ***If*** *(mod(j,2)==0)* **Then**
5\. $KI\ (i, j) = mod(X(p) \times 10^{14}),256)$
6\. ***Else***
7\. $KI(\ i, j) = mod(X(p) \times 10^{14}),256)$
8\. ***End***
9\. ***End***
10\. **For** *i=1 to M*
11\. **For** *j=1 to N* **Do**
12\. $BI(i, j) = dec2bin(I'(\ i, j))$
13\. *flipbits = 8 – mod(KI(i, j), 7) // for 8 bit image*
14\. *FI(i ,j) = flipud(BI(i , j), flipbits)*
15\. **End**
16\. **End**
17\. $CI(1,1) = FI(1,1) \oplus KI(1, 1)$
18\. **For** *row =2 to M* **Do**
19\. **For** *col = 2 to N* **Do**
20\. $CI(row,col)=FI(row,col) \oplus$ $previouspixel(CI(row,col)) \oplus KI(row,col)$
21\. **End**
22\. **End**

4.2.3. Decryption Process

The overall reverse execution of the encryption process produces the result of decryption because of the fact that the field structure of Galois domain F=GF(2^), wherein every element is invertible [30]. Chaotic key series X, Y and Key Image (KI) are the same as in the cipher execution. The inverse form of Bits-Flipping, diffusion and permutation methods need to be executed for decryption. The reverse process is expressed in Equations (4.9), (4.10) and (4.11).

$$FI(row, col) = \begin{cases} CI(1,1) \oplus KI(1,1) \\ CI(row, col) \oplus previous(CI(row, col)) \oplus KI(row, col) \end{cases}$$

(4.9)

$where\ row, col = M, M-1, M-2 \dots 1$

Here, the XOR-ing operation begins from the last pixel of the image and ends in the first pixel. After the reversing process, the flipped image is obtained, and subsequently the reverse Bit-Flipping operation is executed as stated in Equation (4.10).

$$BI(i,j) = convert\ to\ Binary(FI(i,j))$$
$$flipbits = 8 - mod(KI(i,j), 7) \qquad Where\ i,j =$$
$$I'(i,j) = (int)flipud(BI(i,j), flipbits)$$

$1,2,3 \dots M/N$ (4.10)

The confused image will be the result of executing the inverse process of Bits-Flipping. To obtain the plain medical image, a converse process of permutation to be performed by applying similar index values of X and Y chaotic streams as stated in Equation (4.4), then the plain medical image is gained by implementing Equation (4.11) as stated below.

$$PI_{i,j} <=> I'_{IX(i),IY(i)}\ Where, i,j = 1,2,3 \dots M/N \quad (4.11)$$

Finally, the lossless decrypted image PI is obtained.

4.3. Simulation Results and Analysis

Twelve standard test images (eight 8-bit images with size (256 × 256) and four 16-bit CT scan images with size (512 × 512) are taken from S. Barre: medical Imaging: Samples and OSIRIX DICOM Image Library for analysis as shown in Figure 4.4. The proposed cryptosystem for medical image is implemented using MATLAB 2016a with keys k = {X_0 =

0.35678556782345, Y_0 = 0.53456765785432, α = 1234567891011 and β = 110987654321}. Key size, differential, statistical, key sensitivity, and cipher image attacks are executed to assess the image cryptosystem's strength and efficiency. The results are compared with the results obtained from other similar existing solutions currently available.

4.3.1. Statistical Analysis

4.3.1.1. Histogram analysis

The histogram analysis displays the pixel scattering in a graphical form. The randomness of the image cryptosystem is decided by the uniform scattering of pixel values of the cipher image [31].

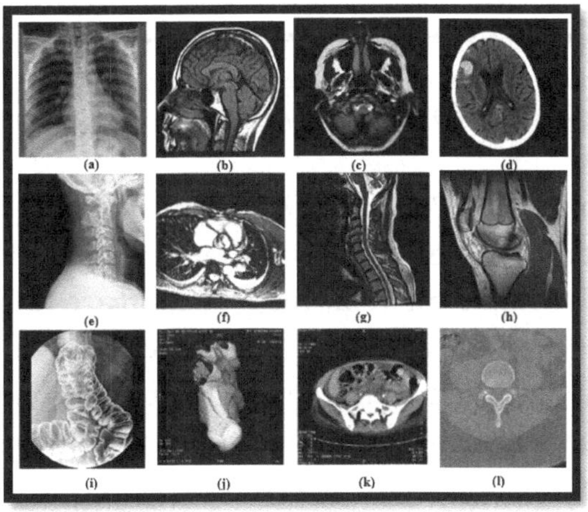

Figure ***Error! No text of specified style in document.****.4 : Sample medical images: (a-h) 256 x 256 (8-bit image), (i-l) 512 x 512 (16-bit image)*

Figure 4.5 depicts the histogram of original and cipher images. Based on analysis and comparison, the histogram results show a uniform scattering in the intensity of the encrypted image. Hence, an advanced cryptosystem offers optimal security to withstand statistical attacks.

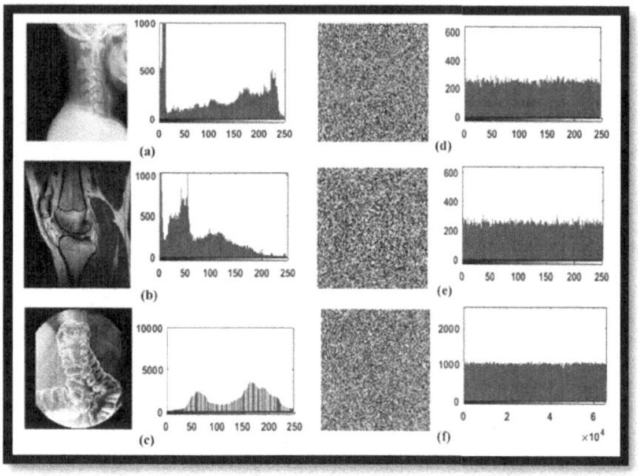

Figure 4.5 : Histogram Analysis: (a, b and c) Original image and its histogram (d, e and f) Corresponding cipher image and its histogram

4.3.1.2. Correlation Coefficient Analysis

Correlation coefficient analysis is one of the most efficient ways to determine the robustness of an image cryptosystem [12]. It helps to calculate the correlation among the neighbouring pixels. All the adjacent pixels are highly interconnected in the plain image. Proposed cryptosystem aims to minimize such association among the pixels and obtain the correlation results of cipher image as zero or nearest to zero.

Table 4.1 presents the correlation coefficients (CC) and the results of different 8-bit encrypted images of size 256 × 256. The obtained results are compared with the cryptosystem [32]. In [32], the algorithm is executed for 30 iterations to achieve a good security level. However, the proposed cryptosystem achieved this level of security in the fifth iteration itself.

Test Images	Proposed Scheme			Enayatifar et.al [32]		
	Horizontal	Vertical	Diagonal	Horizontal	Vertical	Diagonal
	Image size 256 x 256 (8-bit)					
Figure 4.4(a)	7.3857e-04	0.0012	0.0038	0.0127	0.0068	0.0028
Figure 4.4(b)	0.0070	0.0021	0.0040	0.0046	0.0059	0.0041
Figure 4.4(c)	0.0023	-0.0040	0.0042	0.0083	0.0147	0.0016
Figure 4.4(d)	0.0034	-0.0012	-0.0060	0.0142	0.0079	0.0057
Figure 4.4(e)	0.0068	-0.0044	-7.9040e-04	0.0158	0.0115	0.0086
Figure 4.4(f)	0.0030	-8.5079e-04	0.0048	0.0029	0.0031	0.0013
Figure 4.4(g)	0.0018	0.0040	-8.2691e-04	0.0084	0.0062	0.0021
Figure 4.4(h)	0.0017	-0.0042	0.0017	0.0061	0.0097	0.0019
	Image size 512 x 512 (16-bit)			Lima et al. [33]		
Figure 4.4(i)	0.0049	7.4192e-04	-0.0023	0.0032	0.0016	-0.0071
Figure 4.4(j)	7.5681e-04	2.7536e-04	-8.1239e-04	0.0132	0.0056	-0.0006
Figure 4.4(k)	1.1443e-04	-2.9991e-04	-0.0018	0.0012	-0.0003	-0.0087
Figure 4.4(l)	-0.0043	-0.0041	0.0020	-0.0028	-0.0029	0.0007

Table 4.1: Comparison of CC Results with Existing State of the Art

The obtained results are compared in Table 4.1. The proposed cryptosystem performs equally well for 16-bit DICOM images. In the same Table 4.1, a comparison of CC with [33] for image size 512 × 512 (16-bit image) is shown. A comparison of the results shows that the suggested image cryptosystem helps to reduce the correlation among the adjacent pixels in all directions considerably. Consequently, it has good robustness against statistical attacks.

4.3.1.3. Information Entropy

This method is used to determine the level of pixel randomness in a cipher image. The entropy result of the chaotic image is 8. An effective image cryptosystem must produce an entropy result close to 8. However, global entropy does not quantify the actual randomness of encrypted images. Wu et al. [34] specify three flaws of global entropy: inexactness, instability, and inefficiency. To overcome these flaws, they introduced a novel metric known as Local Shannon Entropy (LSE). In LSE, exact randomness is computed using the simple average of the Shannon entropy of non-overlapping cipher image blocks. The local and global entropy results of different cipher images are presented in Table 4.2. In Table 4.2, K represents the number of blocks, and TB denotes the number of picture elements in each block. The results show that both the global and local entropy of the cipher images are close to 8. Hence, the proposed cryptosystem generates highly randomized cipher information.

Test Images	Global Entropy	Local entropy	Local Entropy Critical Values $K = 30, \quad T_B^{L=256*} = 1936$		
			$h_{left}^{l+0.05} = 7.9019$ $h_{right}^{l+0.05} = 7.9030$	$h_{left}^{l+0.01} = 7.9017$ $h_{right}^{l+0.01} = 7.9032$	$h_{left}^{l+0.001} = 7.9015$ $h_{right}^{l+0.001} = 7.9034$
Figure 4.4 (a)	7.9971	7.9085	Passed	Passed	Passed
Figure 4.4 (b)	7.9976	7.9088	Passed	Passed	Passed
Figure 4.4 (c)	7.9972	7.9079	Passed	Passed	Passed
Figure 4.4 (d)	7.9970	7.9072	Passed	Passed	Passed
Figure 4.4 (e)	7.9974	7.9067	Passed	Passed	Passed
Figure 4.4 (f)	7.9971	7.9069	Passed	Passed	Passed
Figure 4.4 (g)	7.9973	7.9066	Passed	Passed	Passed
Figure 4.4 (h)	7.9972	7.9061	Passed	Passed	Passed

Table 4.2: Results of Global and Local Shannon Entropy of Different Test Images

4.3.2. Key Space and Key Sensitivity Analysis

The 2D CCM is developed with the intent of overcoming the drawbacks of a lesser keyspace in the cross-chaotic system. In the proposed scheme, four secret keys {xo, yo, α, β} are used, and the size of each key can reach the maximum value of α×β× 〚10〛 ^28, with xo and yo having a precision value of 〚10〛 ^(-14). A SHA-256 bit key is also taken as a secret key.

Thus, the key size is sufficient to withstand brute force attacks.

Apart from the key size, key sensitivity is an essential element in building a cryptosystem. A robust image cipher should be highly sensitive to the keys [35]. A small change in the key set produces an entirely different cipher image. Hence, key sensitivity analysis is substantial because some parts of the original image can be identified from the detected cipher image by guessing certain exact partial keys.

To illustrate key sensitivity, the test image in Figure 4.6(a) is encrypted with four keys having minor differences, as shown in Table 4.3. The differences between all the cipher image pairs are calculated and shown in Table 4.3. This demonstrates that the new cryptosystem has a high sensitivity to even minor changes in keys.

Keys	**Secret Keys**				**Difference in (%)**			
	X_0	Y_0	α	β	**Key1**	**Key2**	**Key3**	**Key4**
Key1	0.3567855 6882345	0.5345676 5785432	1234567 891011	1110987 654321	-	99.09	99.59	99.52
Key2	0.3567855 6782346	0.5345676 5785432	1234567 891011	1110987 654321	99.09	-	99.15	99.63
Key3	0.3567855 6782346	0.5345676 5785436	1234567 891011	1110987 654321	99.59	99.15	-	99.54
Key4	0.3567855 6782345	0.5345676 5786432	1234567 891012	1110987 654321	99.52	99.64	99.54	-

Table 4.3: Key Sensitivity Analysis

4.3.3. Visualizing Key Sensitivity Analysis

To visualize key sensitivity analysis, 50 pixels are chosen from three encrypted images of the original image in Figure 4.4(a). This image is encrypted using key1, key2, and key3 and their pixels are plotted in Figure 4.6 that points out the dissimilarities. From the results in Figure 4.6 and Table 4.3, it can be seen that there are no identifiable similarities or correlation between the cipher images. Hence, the present cryptosystem has higher key sensitivity.

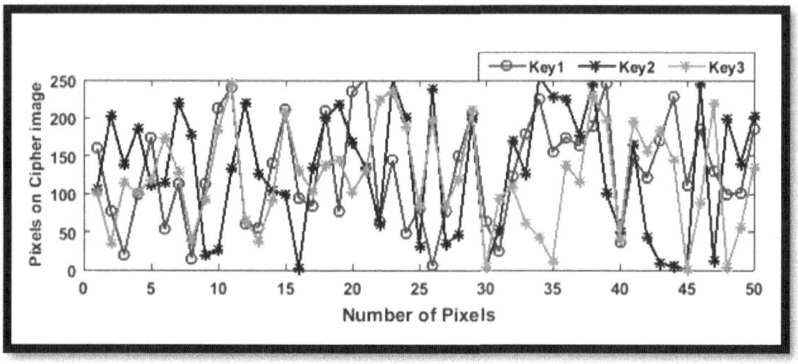

Figure 4.6: Key Sensitivity Analysis: Plot of Three Encrypted Images Using Key1, Key 2 and Key3

4.3.4. Differential Attack Analysis for Security Assessment

Security assessment based on differential analysis of an image cipher uses two qualitative measures, namely NPCR and UACI [10]. These are measures calculated between two cipher images obtained with single bit changes in the same plain image. From Table 4.4, it can be seen the NPCR values of all the images are > 99.67, and the UACI values are >33.45. The comparison of the results proves that the new method produces optimal results and better than [32], [33] and it has the ability to withstand differential attacks.

Test Images		Proposed Scheme			Ref [32]	
		NPCR	UACI		NPCR	UACI
256 x 256 images						
Figure 4.4(a)		0.995803	0.335528		0.990817	0.331845
Figure 4.4(b)		0.996093	0.335440		0.990106	0.331286
Figure 4.4(c)		0.995803	0.335528		0.989251	0.331062
Figure 4.4(d)		0.995789	0.333802		0.994825	0.330473
Figure 4.4(e)		0.996806	0.336161		0.992490	0.333004
Figure 4.4(f)		0.996261	0.332902		0.992592	0.331834
Figure 4.4(g)		0.996338	0.337221		0.989206	0.331169
Figure 4.4(h)		0.992111	0.335237		0.991483	0.331377
512 x 512 images					Ref [33]	
Figure 4.4(i)		99.9977	33.4384		99.6330	33.5556
Figure 4.4(j)		99.9954	33.3395		99.6395	33.5454
Figure 4.4(k)		99.9977	33.3520		99.9939	33.4150
Figure 4.4 (l)		99.9934	33.3769		99.9931	33.4182

*Table **Error! No text of specified style in document.**.2 : Results and Comparison of NPCR and UACI Metrics*

4.3.5. Evaluation Metrics of Encryption and Decryption Quality

The 2D CCM is developed with the intent of overcoming the drawbacks of a smaller keyspace in the cross-chaotic system. In the proposed scheme, four secret keys {xo, yo, α, β} are used, and the size of each key can reach the maximum value of α×β× ⟦10⟧ ^28, with xo and yo having a precision value of ⟦10⟧ ^(-14). A SHA-256 bit key is also taken as a secret key. Thus, the key size is sufficient to withstand brute-force attacks.

Apart from the key size, key sensitivity is an essential element in building a cryptosystem. A robust image cipher should be highly sensitive to the keys [35]. A small change in the key set produces an entirely different cipher image. Hence, key sensitivity analysis is substantial because some parts of the original image can be identified from the detected cipher image by guessing certain exact partial keys.

To illustrate key sensitivity, the test image in Figure 4.6(a) is encrypted with four keys having minor differences, as shown in Table 4.3. The differences between all the cipher image pairs are calculated and shown in Table 4.3. This demonstrates that the new cryptosystem has high sensitivity to even minor changes in keys.

Test Images		Encryption Quality					Decryption Quality			
		CC	MSE	PSNR	SSIM		CC	MSE	PSNR	SSIM
Figure 4.4(a)		-0.0023	8.6941e+03	8.7386	0.0094		1	0	∞	1
Figure 4.4(b)		0.0033	1.4436e+04	6.5365	0.0072		1	0	∞	1
Figure 4.4(c)		0.0012	1.7091e-04	5.8030	0.0024		1	0	∞	1
Figure 4.4(d)		-0.0023	1.6851e+04	5.8645	0.0049		1	0	∞	1
Figure 4.4(e)		8.6072e-04	1.3256e+04	6.9066	0.0063		1	0	∞	1
Figure 4.4(f)		-5.9483e-04	1.3805e+04	6.7303	0.0065		1	0	∞	1
Figure 4.4(g)		-0.0027	1.5933e-04	6.1077	0.0054		1	0	∞	1
Figure 4.4(h)		-0.0015	1.2087e+04	7.3077	0.0059		1	0	∞	1
Figure 4.4(i)		9.0315e-04	1.4298e+09	4.7767	7.5985e-05		1	0	∞	1
Figure 4.4(j)		0.0025	1.4229e-09	4.7976	4.2435e-05		1	0	∞	1
Figure 4.4(k)		-2.1542e-04	1.3878e+09	4.9062	5.1463e-04		1	0	∞	1
Figure 4.4(l)		6.5032e-04	1.3672e-09	4.9713	7.2468e-04		1	0	∞	1

Table 4.5: Parameters of Encryption and Decryption Quality

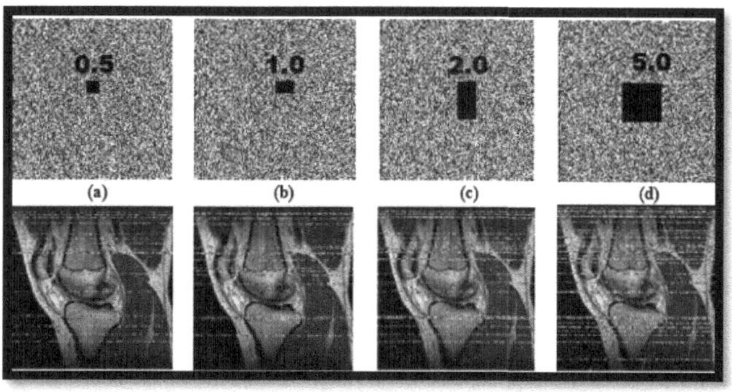

*Figure **Error! No text of specified style in document.**.5 : Crop attack analysis: Cipher image with (a) 0.5% Data Loss (b) 1.0 % Data Loss (c) 2.0% Data Loss (d) 5.0% Data Loss (e, f, g and h) Decrypted images of corresponding cropped cipher image (a, b, c and d)*

4.4. *Computational Complexity Analysis*

The computational complexity of the image with size (M×N) is evaluated by counting the number of iterations required to produce the chaotic key series and to execute the confusion and diffusion processes. Two chaotic series of size (M×N)/2 are generated, from which M or N series of X and Y are used for the confusion process. (M×N)/2 series are used for the diffusion process. The overall number of iterations required for key generation is (M×N)/2. The number of pixels scrambled and substituted in the confusion and diffusion processes is 5 × (M×N). Hence, the total computational complexity of the algorithm is ((M×N)/2 + 5(M×N)). When the constant notations are omitted, the total complexity becomes O(M×N). The complexity becomes O (N^2) when M and N are identical.

4.4.1. Comparison of Performance with Existing Methods

This section compares the results obtained from the proposed cryptosystem with existing chaotic-based medical cryptosystems. Enayatifar et al. [32] compared their cryptosystem with three other methods by executing all three methods using the sample image shown in Figure 4.4(d). The results of the proposed method are compared with existing techniques. Table 4.6 lists the results of entropy, CC, NPCR, and UACI of the encrypted image (Figure 4.4(d)) with an image size of (256 × 256, 8-bit) for each algorithm. Since time complexity plays a predominant role in the execution of real-time applications, the developed algorithm outperforms current methods, as presented in Table 4.6. Though Enayatifar et al. [32] achieved lower time complexity, the other security metrics of our proposed method yield better results. Hence, the proposed cryptosystem is perfectly suitable for implementation in real-time applications. The proposed scheme is also tested with (512 × 512) images of 16-bit and compared with the methodology [33] proposed by Lima et al., and the comparison results are tabulated in Table 4.1 and Table 4.4. The graphical representation of the correlation comparison of both types of images is shown in Figure 4.8. From Tables 4.1, 4.4, and 4.6, it can be seen that the new cryptosystem yields superior results compared to current methods and has the ability to resist both statistical and differential attacks.

Algorithm	Correlation Coefficient			Entropy	NPCR	UACI	Time in
	Horizontal	Vertical	Diagonal				(Sec)
Proposed Scheme	0.0030	-8.50e-04	0.0048	7.9971	0.996261	0.332902	4.86s
Enayatifar et al. [32]-A	0.0029	0.0031	0.0013	7.9991	0.992592	0.331834	2.12s
Enayatifar et al. [38]-B	0.0210	0.0149	0.0062	7.9951	0.986273	0.316822	31.80s
Enayatifar et al. [39]-C	0.0106	0.0062	0.0015	7.9983	0.990383	0.329283	16.95s
Abdullah et al. [40]-D	0.0041	0.0039	0.0008	7.9993	0.991074	0.331085	18.52s

Table 4.6: Comparison of Performance Metrics Regarding Statistical and Differential Attacks

In contrast to other medical image cryptosystems presented in [17]–[19], [33], [41], [42], the following appraisals can be empirically deduced about the proposed cryptosystem:

The present work involves less computational complexity than the works presented by Zhou et al. and Xu et al. [41], [42]. For the proposed scheme, the number of pixel swapping operations required for the confusion process is 5 × (M × N), which is better than (8(8 × M × N)) in [41] and (8 × M × N) in [42]. This proves that the recommended scheme involves less computational complexity than the current methods.

The algorithm proposed requires only five rounds to achieve the desired security level, in contrast to [16], which requires fifteen rounds to achieve an equal distribution of ciphered pixels. Fu et al. [17] require two substitution rounds, and in each round, three permutation rounds are used. A good cryptosystem should be fast in real-time applications. If the number of rounds is increased, it directly affects the time complexity [43]. Therefore, the proposed cryptosystem greatly decreases the number of rounds compared to existing systems and achieves a sufficient level of security, as identified by the security analyses.

Algorithms developed by Ravichandran et al. and Satheshkumar et al. [18], [19] use two or more different chaotic maps to achieve a good security level, but the proposed algorithm uses only one chaotic map with a sufficient key size, achieves a desirable security level, and greatly reduces the time complexity. The comparison analysis shows that the present work is far better than the existing methods [17]–[19], [33], [41], [42].

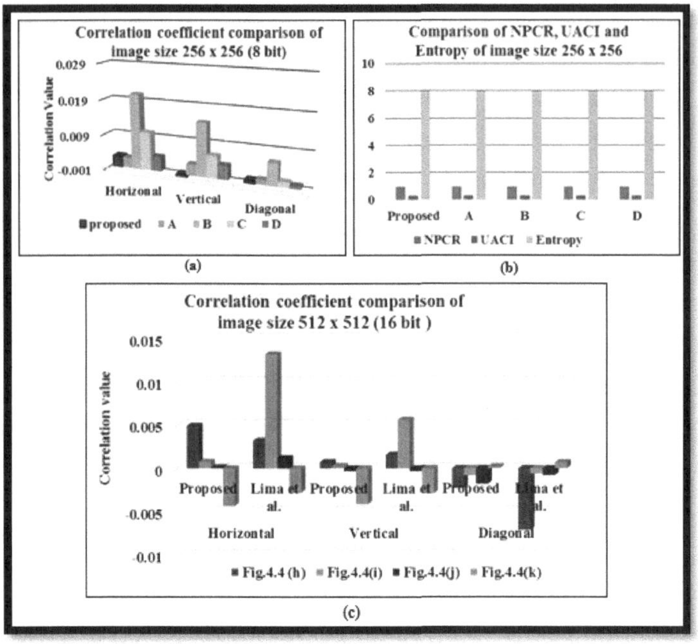

*Figure **Error! No text of specified style in document.**.6 : Graphical Representation for the Comparison Results A) CC B) NPCR, UACI and Entropy C) CC of Image Size 512 X 512*

4.5. Chapter Summary

A secure chaos-based medical image cryptosystem is developed using fusional 2D CCM. The outcome of the NIST test suite demonstrates that the chaotic intervals of 2D CCM are purely random. The graphical representation of the Lyapunov exponent and bifurcation results provides evidence that the 2D CCM is highly sensitive to initial seed keys. Additionally, the proposed dynamic Bit-Flipping technique enhances the security level in the diffusion process. The performance and security of the proposed method are evaluated using statistical attack, differential attack, key sensitivity, and key space analyses. The robustness of the method is proven by carrying out various cipher image attacks and analyzing the results. Comparisons with existing methods make it clear that the proposed cryptosystem produces a well-encrypted image and offers optimal protection for storing and transmitting medical images over insecure networks.

4.6. References

i. Sahi, A., Lai, D., & Li, Y. (2016). Security and privacy preserving approaches in the eHealth clouds with disaster recovery plan. *Computers in Biology and Medicine, 78*, 1–8.

ii. Abdulla, A. A., Sellahewa, H., & Jassim, S. A. (2014). Stego quality enhancement by message size reduction and fibonacci bit-plane mapping. *Lecture Notes in Computer Science (including subseries Lecture Notes in Artificial Intelligence and Lecture Notes in Bioinformatics), 8893*, 151–166.

iii. Bouslimi, D., Coatrieux, G., & Roux, C. (2011). A joint encryption/watermarking algorithm for verifying the reliability of medical images: Application to echographic. *Computers in Biology and Medicine, 16*(5), 1–8.

iv. Khashan, O. A., & Alshaikh, M. (2020). Edge-based lightweight selective encryption scheme for digital medical images. *pp. 26369–26388.*

v. Identity Theft Resource Center (ITRC). (2019). https://www.idtheftcenter.org/wp-content/uploads/2020/01/01.28.2020_ITRC_2019-End-of-Year-Data-Breach-Report_FINAL.

vi. Abdulla, A. A. (2015). Exploiting similarities between secret and cover images for improved embedding efficiency and security in digital steganography. *no. October*.

vii. Liu, H., Wen, F., & Kadir, A. (2019). Construction of a new 2D Chebyshev-Sine map and its application to color image encryption. *Multimedia Tools and Applications, 78*(12), 15997–16010.

viii. Xu, C., Sun, J., & Wang, C. (2020). A novel image encryption algorithm based on bit-plane matrix rotation and hyper chaotic systems. *Multimedia Tools and Applications, 79*(9–10), 5573–5593.

ix. Chai, X., Zheng, X., Gan, Z., & Chen, Y. (2020). Exploiting plaintext-related mechanism for secure color image encryption. *Neural Computing and Applications, 32*(12), 8065–8088.

x. Elashry, I. F., et al. (2020). Efficient chaotic-based image cryptosystem with different modes of operation. *Multimedia Tools and Applications, 79*(29–30), 20665–20687.

xi. Faragallah, O. S., et al. (2020). Secure color image cryptosystem based on chaotic logistic in the FrFT domain. *Multimedia Tools and Applications, 79*(3–4), 2495–2519.

xii. Guesmi, R., & Ben Farah, M. A. (2020). A new efficient medical image cipher based on hybrid chaotic map and DNA code.

xiii. Idrees, B., Zafar, S., Rashid, T., & Gao, W. (2020). Image encryption algorithm using S-box and dynamic Hénon bit level permutation. *Multimedia Tools and Applications, 79*(9–10), 6135–6162.

xiv. Vidhya, R., & Brindha, M. (2020). A novel dynamic chaotic image encryption using butterfly network topology based diffusion and decision based permutation. *Multimedia Tools and Applications.*

xv. Hua, Z., Yi, S., & Zhou, Y. (2018). Medical image encryption using high-speed scrambling and pixel adaptive diffusion. *Signal Processing, 144*, 134–144.

xvi. Hu, J., & Han, F. (2009). A pixel-based scrambling scheme for digital medical images protection. *Journal of Network and Computer Applications, 32*(4), 788–794.

xvii. Fu, C., et al. (2013). An efficient and secure medical image protection scheme based on chaotic maps. *Computers in Biology and Medicine, 43*(8), 1000–1010.

xviii. Ravichandran, D., Praveenkumar, P., Balaguru Rayappan, J. B., & Amirtharajan, R. (2016). Chaos based crossover and mutation for securing DICOM image. *Computers in Biology and Medicine, 72*, 170–184.

xix. Sathishkumar, G. A., Bhoopathybagan, K., Sriraam, N., Venkatachalam, S. P., & Vignesh, R. (2011). A novel image encryption algorithm using two chaotic maps for medical application. *Communications in Computer and Information Science, 133*(3), 290–299.

xx. Mondal, B., Behera, P. K., & Gangopadhyay, S. (2020). A secure image encryption scheme based on a novel 2D sine–cosine cross-chaotic (SC3) map. *Journal of Real-Time Image Processing.*

xxi. Liu, Y., Qin, Z., Liao, X., & Wu, J. (2020). Cryptanalysis and enhancement of an image encryption scheme based on a 1-D coupled Sine map. *Nonlinear Dynamics, 100*(3), 2917–2931.

xxii. Huang, R., Liao, X., Dong, A., & Sun, S. (2020). Cryptanalysis and security enhancement for a chaos-based color image encryption algorithm. *Multimedia Tools and Applications.*

xxiii. Wang, H., Xiao, D., Chen, X., & Huang, H. (2018). Cryptanalysis and enhancements of image encryption using combination of the 1D chaotic map. *Signal Processing, 144*, 444–452.

xxiv. Tan, C. H., Prabowo, T. F., & Le, D. (2016). Breaking an ID-based encryption based on discrete logarithm and factorization problems. *Information Processing Letters, 116*(2), 116–119.

xxv. Bechikh, R., Hermassi, H., El-latif, A. A. A., Rhouma, R., & Belghith, S. (2015). Breaking an image encryption scheme based on a spatiotemporal chaotic system. *Signal Processing: Image Communication, 39*, 151–158.

xxvi. Chen, J., Chen, L., Zhang, L. Y., & Zhu, Z. L. (2019). Medical image cipher using hierarchical diffusion and non-sequential encryption. *Nonlinear Dynamics, 96*(1), 301–322.

xxvii. Chai, X., Zhang, J., Gan, Z., & Zhang, Y. (2019). Medical image encryption algorithm based on Latin square and memristive chaotic system. *Multimedia Tools and Applications, 78*(24), 35419–35453.

xxviii. Stalin, S., Maheshwary, P., Shukla, P. K., Maheshwari, M., Gour, B., & Khare, A. (2019). Fast and Secure Medical Image Encryption Based on Non Linear 4D Logistic Map and DNA Sequences (NL4DLM_DNA). *Journal of Medical Systems, 43*(8).

xxix. Kessler, G. (2012). *Byte logic table.* https://www.garykessler.net/library/byte_logic_table.html

xxx. Benvenuto, C. J. (2012). Galois Field in Cryptography. *pp. 1–11.*

xxxi. Rajendran, S., Krithivasan, K., & Doraipandian, M. (2020). Fast pre-processing hex Chaos triggered color image cryptosystem. *Multimedia Tools and Applications, 12447–12469.*

xxxii. Nematzadeh, H., Enayatifar, R., Motameni, H., Guimarães, F. G., & Coelho, V. N. (2018). Medical image encryption using a hybrid model of modified genetic algorithm and coupled map lattices. *Optics and Lasers in Engineering, 110*, 24–32.

xxxiii. Lima, J. B., Madeiro, F., & Sales, F. J. R. (2015). Encryption of medical images based on the cosine number transform. *Signal Processing: Image Communication, 35*, 1–8.

xxxiv. Wu, Y., Zhou, Y., Saveriades, G., Agaian, S., & Noonan, J. P. (2013). Local Shannon entropy measure with statistical tests for image randomness. *Information Sciences, 222*, 323–342.

xxxv. Ali, T. S., & Ali, R. (2020). A Novel Medical Image Signcryption Scheme Using TLTS and Henon Chaotic Map. *IEEE Access, 8*, 71974–71992.

xxxvi. Patro, K. A. K., & Acharya, B. (2020). A novel multi-dimensional multiple image encryption technique. *Multimedia Tools and Applications, 79*(19–20), 12959–12994.

i. Talhaoui, M. Z., Wang, X., & Midoun, M. A. (2020). Fast image encryption algorithm with high security level using the Bülban chaotic map. *Journal of Real-Time Image Processing*.

ii. Abdullah, A. H., Enayatifar, R., & Lee, M. (2012). A hybrid genetic algorithm and chaotic function model for image encryption. *AEU - International Journal of Electronics and Communications, 66*(10), 806–816.

iii. Enayatifar, R., Abdullah, A. H., & Lee, M. (2013). A weighted discrete imperialist competitive algorithm (WDICA) combined with chaotic map for image encryption. *Optics and Lasers in Engineering, 51*(9), 1066–1077.

iv. Enayatifar, R., Hanan, A., & Isnin, I. F. (2014). Chaos-based image encryption using a hybrid genetic algorithm and a DNA sequence. *Optics and Lasers in Engineering, 56*, 83–93.

v. Zhou, Y., Cao, W., & Chen, C. L. P. (2014). Image encryption using binary bitplane. *Signal Processing, 100*, 197–207.

vi. Xu, L., Li, Z., Li, J., & Hua, W. (2016). A novel bit-level image encryption algorithm based on chaotic maps. *Optics and Lasers in Engineering, 78*, 17–25.

vii. Wang, X., Zhao, H., & Wang, M. (2019). A new image encryption algorithm with nonlinear-diffusion based on Multiple coupled map lattices. *Optics and Laser Technology, 115*, 42–57.

CHAPTER 5

Fast Pre-processing Hex Chaos Triggered Color Image Cryptosystem

5.1. Introduction

Plenty of conventional encryption algorithms are available for the secure transmission and storage of images. Among them, chaos-based image cryptosystems have proven to be efficient due to their outstanding inbuilt features, such as sensitivity to seed keys, determinism, ergodicity, and randomness. Even though numerous 1D and 2D chaotic map-based image cryptosystems have been developed, these maps are not sufficient for color images because of their large size and redundancy across three separate channels (Red, Blue, and Green). Zheng et al. [1] specified that even though most lower-dimensional chaos-based image cryptosystems have achieved satisfactory results, these chaotic systems have two main drawbacks—limited random periods of chaotic series and lower key space, which is insufficient to resist different attacks. Many lower-dimensional image cryptosystems have been cryptanalyzed [2]–[4].

Higher-dimensional (3D, 4D, 5D, etc.) hyper-chaotic maps overcome these drawbacks by offering desirable features such as higher randomness, longer periodicity, and a higher range of positive Lyapunov exponents [5]–[9]. Kadir et al. [10] designed a coupled hyper-chaotic system by combining two Lorenz chaotic systems and generating six chaotic sequences for encrypting color images. Guodong Ye et al. [11] suggested chaotic image encryption by combining a

3D Arnold cat map and a logistic map, with the SHA-3 function employed to generate an initial key from the plain image to resist known-plaintext attacks. Li et al. [12] introduced a five-dimensional hyper-chaotic system and adapted a combination of pixel-level and bit-level permutation to improve image security. Chai et al. [13] proposed a dynamic DNA image cryptosystem by utilizing a four-wing hyper-chaotic system, which has highly random behavior and a large key space to resist brute force attacks, while SHA-384 is employed to generate initial values of the chaotic system, allowing the cryptosystem to resist known/chosen plaintext attacks. Girdhar et al. [14] developed a new Rossler-Lorenz 3D hyper-chaotic map, and the key series generated by this map was utilized in the DNA cryptosystem to encrypt the image.

In all the scenarios discussed above, the number of generated chaotic series should be equal to the size of the original image, and all chaotic series need to be converted from decimal form to integers to perform arithmetic or logical operations between the chaotic series and the image to obtain the encrypted image. Some arithmetic and modulo operations are executed on each decimal-form chaotic series to convert them to an applicable integer form. Due to this, encryption algorithms require considerable memory space and time, making the cryptosystems lack performance and efficiency.

Hence, considering the above issue, a new pre-processing technique is proposed using the hexadecimal system, with bit-level permutation based on hex chaotic series. The main contribution of this work is to reduce pre-processing time while increasing performance and security levels. In the proposed pre-processing method, four hexadecimal values are obtained from a single chaotic value, significantly reducing the required number of chaotic series—only ¼ of the original image size is needed. Accordingly, the proposed cryptosystem requires less computation time, memory space, and is faster than earlier techniques. In terms of security, the developed cryptosystem adopts bit-level merging and circular shifting, which depend on chaotic keys in the diffusion process, enhancing security. The 4D Lorenz chaotic system is used to generate the chaotic series for the proposed cryptosystem.

5.2. *Lorenz Hyper-Chaotic System*

It is a well-known fact that a robust cryptosystem should have a large key space and high key sensitivity to resist various attacks. Since hyper-chaotic systems possess large key spaces, they provide high security. One of the most familiar hyper-chaotic systems is the Lorenz hyper-chaotic system [15], described in Equation (5.1) where x_0, y_0, z_0 & $w_0 \in (0, 1]$ are initial parameters

$$\left\{\begin{array}{ll} \dot{x} = a(y-x)+w & a, a = 10 \\ \dot{y} = cx - y - xz & b, b = \frac{8}{3} \\ \dot{z} = xy - bz & c, c > 24.74 \\ \dot{w} = -yz + rw & r, -1.52 \le r \le -0.06 \end{array}\right\} \begin{array}{c} System \\ Parameters \end{array} \quad (5.1)$$

The system exhibits chaotic behaviour only in the above mentioned ranges of system and initial parameters. In order to illustrate the chaotic behaviour of the hyper Lorenz map, the proposed scheme chosen the initial values as x_0= 0.2551, y_0= 1.3572, z_0= 0.253, w_0= 0.2344, and the system parameter values are set as c=28.0 and r= -1.0. The randomness of the generated chaotic series is concluded by the chaotic attractors, which are illustrated in Figure 5.1.

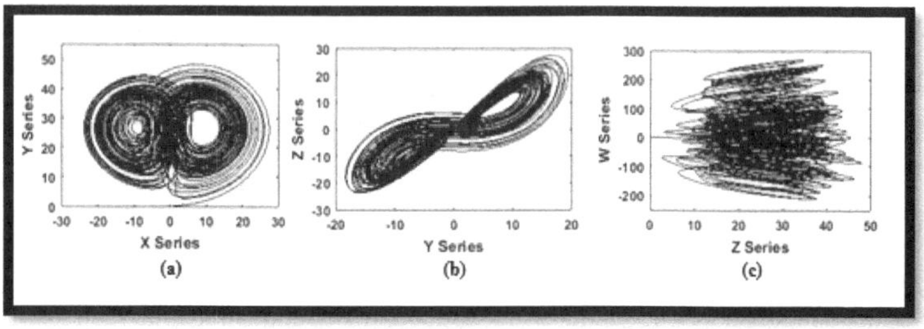

Figure 5.1: Chaotic Attractor of Lorenz Hyper Chaotic Map A) X_Y Phase B) Y_Z Phase C) Z_W Phase

5.3. Hyper Hexadecimal System Based Key Generation

Chaotic sequences generated by chaotic maps are in the form of decimal values. In the confusion process, the array index values of the sorted chaotic series are used, so there is no need for conversion. However, in diffusion, the chaotic series need to be applied for some arithmetic or logical operations with pixel values of the image, so the decimal value chaotic series cannot be applied directly. As pixel values of the images are in integer form, the chaotic sequences should be converted for computational purposes. Zhang *et al.* [16] truncated the precision values and used only the real part of the chaotic sequences. In some papers, the authors used arithmetic and modulo operations to convert the decimal form to integer form [14], [17], [18]. These types of conversions are easily recognized by intruders, so they can easily hack the key series by performing some statistical attacks. The proposed method uses hexadecimal values of chaotic series to convert the decimal value chaotic series to integer form. The final integer chaotic key streams are used for diffusion. The procedure of key generation based on hexadecimal system is illustrated in Algorithm 3.

5.3.1. Algorithm 3: Generation of chaotic key series using hyper hexadecimal system

Four chaotic series are generated from Lorenz system, these series are converted to integer form by executing the following steps.

Step 1: Generate four chaotic series X, Y, Z, and W using Lorenz hyper chaotic map of size $(N \times M)/8$ defined in Equation (5.2).

$$\begin{cases} X = \{x_1, x_2, x_3 \dots\dots x_{size}\}\ Y = \{y_1, y_2, y_3 \dots\dots y_{size}\} \\ Z = \{z_1, z_2, z_3 \dots\dots z_{size}\}\ W = \{w_1, w_2, w_3 \dots\dots w_{size}\} \end{cases} \quad (5.2)$$

Where N and M represent the height and width of the image and size = $(N \times M)/8$

Step 2: Convert each chaotic key series into Hexa-Decimal (HD) values. The conversion is done by using num2hex() function in Matlab defined in Equation (5.3).

$$\begin{cases} X' = num2hex(X)\ Y' = num2hex(Y) \\ Z' = num2hex(Z)\ W' = num2hex(W) \end{cases} \quad (5.3)$$

Step 3: Each 16 digit HD value is fragmented into four different HD values, for example, if the input image size is (256×256) then, each chaotic series is generated for $(256 \times 256)/8$ times i.e. 8192 series. After HD conversion, 8192 HD values (16 digits) are obtained for each series. Fragmentation is applied to each HD value. As a result, $8192 \times 4 = 32768$ HD series are achieved, which is equal to ½ the image size (256×256). Detailed illustration of fragmentation is shown in Figure 5.2 and shortly described in Equation (5.4).

$$\begin{cases} X'' = Fragmentation(X')\ Y'' = Fragmentation(Y') \\ Z'' = Fragmentation(Z')\ W'' = Fragmentation(W') \end{cases} \quad (5.4)$$

Step 4: Each of the four digit HD values is converted into integer form by performing a modulo operation between each HD value with one of the keys, which specify the number of blocks that image has to be divided for the diffusion process. The module operation by using the mkey is represented in Equation (5.5), and the example conversion of two chaotic values is given in Figure 5.2.

$$\begin{cases} IX = mod(X'', mkey)\ IY = mod(Y'', mkey) \\ IZ = mod(Z'', mkey)\ IW = mod(W'', mkey) \end{cases} \quad (5.5)$$

If key = {4, 8, 16, 32} then mkey = {32, 64, 128, 256}

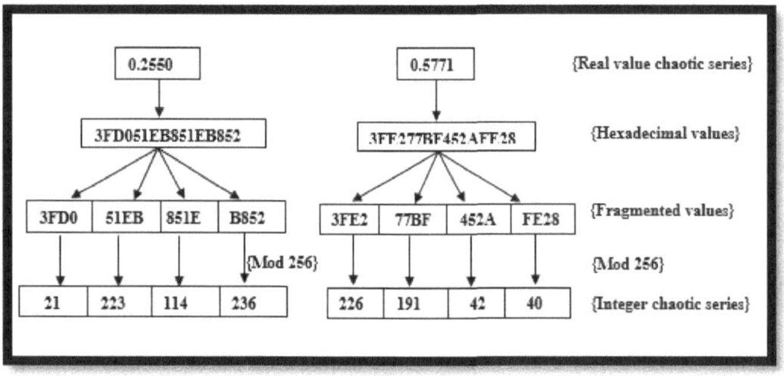

Figure ***Error! No text of specified style in document.***.*7 : Generation of Integer Chaotic Series Using Hexadecimal Conversion and Fragmentation*

To illustrate the randomness of the converted chaotic series, the first 1,000 key series are taken from IX, and their randomness is proven by plotting the chaotic series, as shown in Figure 5.3. Entropy is another metric used to measure the level of randomness. The approximate random image entropy rate is 8. Hence, the entropy level is calculated for four integer-format chaotic series, and the results obtained for the entropy of IX and IY are 7.8870 and 7.8964, while the entropy of IZ and IW is 7.7567 and 7.8870. All these results are close to 8, so all the series have sufficient randomness. The chaotic behavior of the map is maintained even after the conversion.

5.4. Comparison of Pre-Processing with Existing Techniques

Pre-processing is required to convert decimal form chaotic series into integer form in the diffusion process of the chaos based cryptosystems. In most existing schemes, a combination of different arithmetic and modulo operations are utilized for pre-processing, and the size of chaotic series need to convert should be equal to the size of the input image. So, processing time and memory required for pre-processing is higher in those existing schemes. But, in the proposed system, the required size of chaotic series need to convert is ¼ of input image size, pre-processing utilizes only simple hexadecimal conversion and mod operation. So, the processing time and memory are less compared to existing schemes. Table 5.1 compares the number of chaotic series required for pre-processing, processing time and memory allocated for key generation and pre-processing between existing and proposed scheme. The pre-processing functions are executed in MATLAB 2016b on a PC with 16GB Memory, 250 GB hard disk, 2.4 GHz Intel core 2 Duo processor. From Table 5.1, it can be realized that the proposed pre-processing method is faster and utilized less memory than the existing scheme. Hence, it increases the overall performance of the encryption algorithm.

pre-processing function	No. of. PP	PT	Memory used (Kb)
Ref. [14] $X = ((abs(X) - floor(X)10^{14}) \times mod2^{10}$	$4 \times (M \times N)$	7.411	1792
Ref. [18] $X = fix(mod\left(\left(abs(X) - floor\left(abs(X)\right)\right) \times 10^{14}, 256\right))$	$4 \times (M \times N)$	7.385	2824
Ref. [19] $X = ((10^3) \times (X)) - round(10^3 \times (X))$	$3 \times (M \times N)$	5.783	2328
Proposed pre-processing function	$4 \times ((M \times N)/8)$	4.517	1276

*Table **Error! No text of specified style in document.**.3 : Comparison of Key Series Generation: Number of Pre-Processing (No. Of. PP) Processing Time (PT) and Memory between Proposed and Existing Systems*

5.5. Image Cryptosystem Based on Hexadecimal Hyper Chaotic Map

The block view of the proposed cryptosystem is presented in Figure 5.4, and its step-by-step procedure is explained as follows.

Step 1: Color Image (CI) of size $(N \times M)$ is taken as input, where N and M specifies the height and width of the input image

Step 2: RGB components of the image are separated and stored in three separate arrays, R, G, and B having the same size as the input image $(N \times M)$

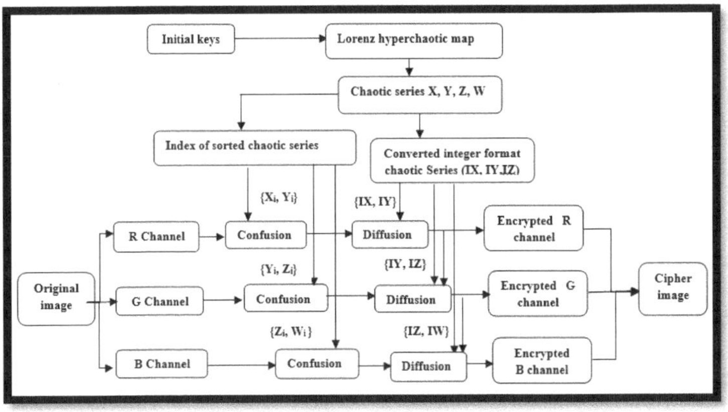

Figure 5.4: Block View of the Proposed Image Cryptosystem

Step 3: Four chaotic series X, Y, Z, W are generated using hyper Lorenz system as follows

$$\begin{cases} X = \{x_1, x_2, x_3 \dots\dots x_{size}\} \; Y = \{y_1, y_2, y_3 \dots\dots y_{size}\} \\ Z = \{z_1, z_2, z_3 \dots\dots z_{size}\} \; W = \{w_1, w_2, w_3 \dots\dots w_{size}\} \end{cases} Where\ size = M \times N/key$$

These chaotic series are sorted, and their new index values are stored separately as shown in Equation (5.6).

$$\begin{cases} [ax, sx] = sort(X_i) \; [ay, sy] = sort(Y_i) \\ [az, sz] = sort(Z_i) \; [aw, sw] = sort(W_i) \end{cases} \{ i = 1,2,3, \dots\dots M/N \quad (5.6)$$

Here, { *ax, ay, az, aw*} are the new sorted sequences of {X_i, Y_i, Z_i *Wi* } and {*sx, sy, sz sw* } are the index values of the new chaotic sequence { *ax, ay, az, aw*}.

Step 4: Using any two pairs of the new index values {*sx, sy, sz, sw*} each component of the image is shuffled. Equation (5.7) illustrates the shuffling process.

$$\begin{cases} R'_{i,j} \leftrightarrow R_{sx(p),sy(q)} \\ G'_{i,j} \leftrightarrow G_{sy(p),sz(q)} \\ B'_{i,j} \leftrightarrow B_{sz(p),sw(q)} \end{cases} \begin{cases} i,j = 1,2,3 \dots M/N, \\ p,q = 1,2,3 \dots M/\,N \end{cases} \quad (5.7)$$

At the end of this step, the RGB components are completely shuffled, and the confused image is obtained, which is given as an input for the diffusion process.

Step 5: Divide the confused components into non-overlapping blocks, the following Matlab code is used to break the image into blocks. Number of blocks can be identified by $(blocks = 2 * (M/key))$.

$$RB = mat2cell\ (R', ones(M/key, 1) \times key, ones(M/key\ , 1) \times key)$$
$$GB = mat2cell\ (G', ones(M/key, 1) \times key, ones(M/key\ , 1) \times key)$$
$$BB = mat2cell\ (B', ones(M/key, 1) \times key, ones(M/key\ , 1) \times key)$$

Step 6: Create three sub key series from X, Y, Z, and W using Equation (5.8) utilized for diffusion operation.

$$K1(i) = X(i)\ if((mod(i, 2)) == 0)\ K2(i) = Y(i)\ if((mod(i, 2)) == 0)$$
$$K1(i) = Y(i)\ if((mod(i, 2)) \neq 0)\quad K2(i) = Z(i)\ if((mod(i, 2)) \neq 0)$$

(5.8)

$$\begin{matrix} K1(i) = Z(i)\ if((mod(i, 2)) == 0) \\ K1(i) = W(i)\ if((mod(i, 2)) \neq 0) \end{matrix}\ Where\ i = 1,2,3 \ldots\ldots size$$

Step 7: Convert each block pixel value of RB, GB, and BB into an 8-bit binary representation, then apply merge and circular shift operation on each row of the blocks. The following Matlab code represents both operations for RB components, and the same code is applied for GB and BB components by using K2 and K3.

$$\begin{matrix} binblocks\{i, j\} = \ dec2bin(RB\{i, j\}, 8) \\ mergerow = reshape(horzcat(binblocks\{k, :\}), 1, [\,]) \\ shiftrow = circshift\big(mergerow, K1(p)\big) \end{matrix} \left\{ \begin{matrix} i, j = 1,2,3 \ldots\ldots blocks \\ k = 1,2,3 \ldots\ldots key \\ p = 1,2,3 \ldots\ldots size \end{matrix} \right.$$

The obtained $shiftrow$ binary values are separated into 8 bits and converted into their corresponding decimal values by using the function $2dec()$. The demonstration of merging and shifting operations of a single 4 x 4 block is shown in Figure.5.5.

Separate pair of two chaotic series among IX, IY, IZ, and IW can be used to diffuse each component of the image. The diffusion process of R, G, and B component are illustrated in Equations (5.9 and 5.10).

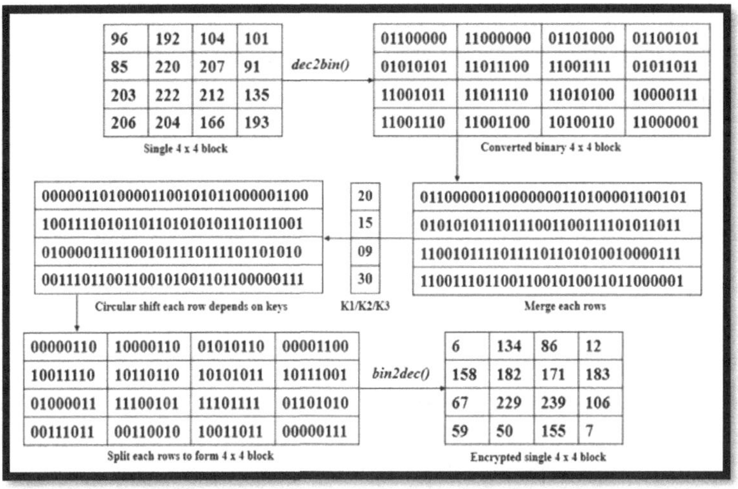

Figure 5.5: Demonstration of Merging and Circular Shift Operation

$$ER = \begin{cases} ER(1,1) = RB(1,1) \\ ER(1,k) = bitxor\big(ER(1,k-1), RB(1,k)\big) \\ ER(i,j) = bitxor(RB(i,j), ER(i,j-1) \end{cases} \begin{cases} k = 2,3, \ldots \ldots M/N \\ i = 1,2,3, \ldots \ldots M/N \\ j = 2,3, \ldots \ldots M/N \end{cases}$$

(5.9)

$$\begin{matrix} EG = (GB(i,j) \oplus prev(GB(i,j) \oplus ER(i,j) \\ EB = bitxor(EB(i,j) \oplus prev(EB(i,j) \oplus EG(i,j) \end{matrix} \{i,j = 1,2,3 \ldots \ldots M/N$$ (5.10)

Step 6: The three components (ER, EG, EB) are merged to create final encrypted image (C). The algorithm for retrieving the plain image (P) is a transposed process of the encryption procedure. Keys are shared in secure form by utilizing some of the key sharing methods [20] [21].

5.6. Decryption Process

The decryption involves a complete inversion of the encryption process. Generation of the chaotic key streams $\{X, Y, Z, W\}$ *and* $\{k1, k2, k3\}$ is common as in the encryption process. At first, the received encrypted image (C) is separated into three components $\{ER, EG, EB\}$ then apply the inverse process of diffusion as given in the following Equation (5.11).

$$RB = \begin{cases} RB(1,1) = ER(1,1) \\ RB(1,k) = bitxor\big(ER(1,k-1), ER(1,k)\big) \\ RB(i,j) = bitxor(ER(i,j), ER(i,j-1) \end{cases} \begin{cases} k = M/N \ldots\ldots 3,2 \\ i = M/N \ldots\ldots 3,2,1 \\ j = M/N \ldots\ldots 3,2 \end{cases}$$

(5.11)

Similarly, Equation (5.11) is applied to $\{EG \ and \ EB\}$ to obtain $\{GB \ and \ BB\}$ after, each component is divided into blocks then apply the inverse circular shift operation by applying the following Matlab code.

$$\begin{matrix} binblocks\{i,j\} = dec2bin(RB\{i,j\}, 8) \\ mergerow = reshape(horzcat(binblocks\{k,:\}), 1, [\,]) \\ shiftrow = circshift\big(mergerow, mkey - k1(p)\big) \end{matrix} \begin{cases} i,j = 1,2,3 \ldots\ldots blocks \\ k = 1,2,3 \ldots\ldots key \\ p = 1,2,3 \ldots\ldots size \end{cases}$$

The obtained $shiftrow$ binary values are separated into 8 bits and converted into their corresponding decimal values by using the function $bin2dec()$. The result of inverse diffusion is obtained by combining the blocks into a single component. Similarly, this process is applied to the other two components GB and BB, to obtain the confused components $\{R', G' \ and \ B'\}$.

To get the original image, an inverse of confusion needs to be executed using the same index value of $\{X, Y, Z \ and \ W\}$ chaotic streams as stated in Equation (5.6) then the original R, G, and B component of image can be obtained by executing Equation (5.12) stated below.

$$\begin{cases} R_{i,j} \leftrightarrow R'_{sx(p),sy(q)} \\ G_{i,j} \leftrightarrow G'_{sy(p),sz(q)} \\ B_{i,j} \leftrightarrow B'_{sz(p),sw(q)} \end{cases} \begin{cases} i,j = 1,2,3 \dots \dots M/N \\ p,q = 1,2,3 \dots \dots M/N \end{cases} \quad (5.12)$$

Finally, a decrypted image P is obtained by concatenating the R, G and B components.

5.7. Experimental Result

The proposed image cryptosystem is illustrated using 24-bit colour images of size 256 X 256 from Signal and Image Processing Institute (SIPI) image database are taken as plain input images [22]. Lorenz hyper chaotic map used to generate key series using initial values and system parameters. These initial and system parameters are utilized as keys. The key values taken for the proposed scheme x_0 = *0.25345233254121*, y_0 = *00054323461231*, z_0 = *0.25678915461235 and* w_0 = *0. 23564532314324* and the system parameter values are a = 10.0, b = 8/3.0, c = 28.0 and r = -1.0. Each component of the input image is confused using any one pair of the chaotic series $X, Y, Z, and\ W$. Then, the confused RGB components are diffused using the combination of any pair of chaotic series. The original images and their corresponding cipher images are shown in Figure 5.6.

5.8. Performance and Security Analysis

5.8.1. Statistical Analysis

Statistical analysis is a crucial investigation method that helps to establish the strength of the proposed cryptosystem against various measurable attacks. The proposed cryptosystem is evaluated using the histogram and the correlation coefficient among the nearby pixels in all directions of the cipher image.

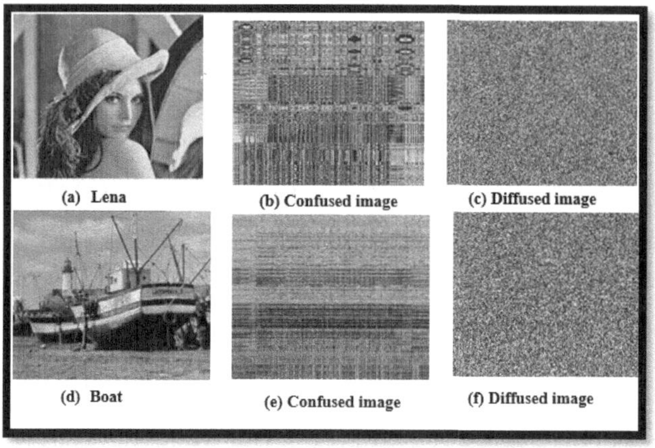

Figure ***Error! No text of specified style in document.****.8 : Experimental Outcome: Original Image and Their Corresponding Confused and Diffused Image*

5.8.2. Histogram Analysis

Histogram analysis acts as a main characteristic to find the amount of uniform distribution of pixels in cipher image [29]. Figure 5.7(a) illustrates the histogram of RGB component of the original pepper image. The distribution of pixels of the cipher image is shown in Figure 5.7(b), which are uniformly distributed to protect the image from statistical attacks

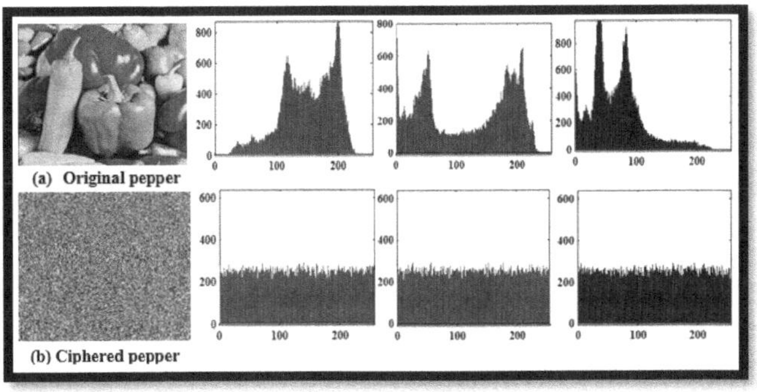

*Figure **Error! No text of specified style in document.**.9 : Histogram Analysis between RGB Components of Original and Ciphered Pepper Image*

5.8.3. Correlation Coefficient Analysis

This analysis calculates the relationship between neighbouring pixels of the image [23]. Each pixel in the original image is highly interconnected with the nearest ones. The main goal of encryption is to reduce such correlation. The correlation results of the original and ciphered image are presented in Figure 5.8, which shows that the proposed cipher has greatly reduced the correlation.

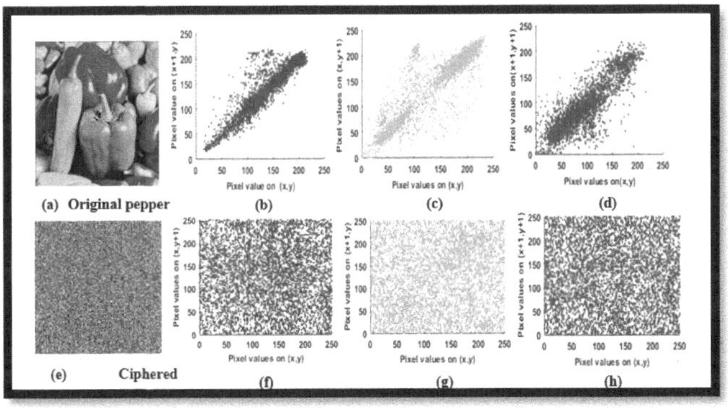

Figure 5.8: Correlation Coefficient Analysis: Correlation of Pixels in (B and F) Horizontal Direction of Red Component (C and G) Vertical Direction of Green Component (D and H) Diagonal Direction of Blue Component

SIPI database images are taken for testing, and their results are shown in Table 5.2. Additionally, the comparison analysis is presented in Table 5.3. These results provide evidence that the proposed cipher has high efficiency in withstanding statistical attacks, and the security level is higher than that of existing image cryptosystems.

5.8.4. Global and Local Information Entropy Analysis

Information entropy is used to illustrate the amount of uncertainty among pixels [24]. A good encryption procedure should have the entropy of the ciphered image close to 8. However, Wu et al. [25] proved that this global entropy analysis is not sufficient to assess the randomness of a ciphered image. They proposed a new metric to evaluate randomness called local Shannon entropy. Here, true randomness is calculated using the simple mean of Shannon entropy of non-overlapping ciphered image blocks. The global and local entropy results of encrypted SIPI color images are tabulated in Table 5.2. It can be seen from the results that global and local entropy achieved the acceptance rate. Consequently, Table 5.3 proves that the global entropy results of the proposed scheme have a better acceptance rate than some existing methodologies.

Test Images	24-bit Encrypted Image Correlation			Global Shannon entropy	Local Shannon entropy	Local entropy critical values K= 30 $T_B^{L=256}$ = 1936
	Horizontal	Vertical	Diagonal			> 7.9015
4.1.01	-0.0048	0.0085	3.8063e^{-04}	7.9963	7.9069	Passed
4.1.02	-9.8780e-04	0.0161	1.9148e^{-04}	7.9957	7.9068	Passed
4.1.03	6.6557 e^{-05}	0.0050	-0.0031	7.9958	7.9073	Passed
4.1.04	-0.0052	0.0058	0.0012	7.9972	7.9087	Passed
4.1.05	0.0031	-0.0011	8.2070 e^{-04}	7.9966	7.9073	Passed
4.1.06	3.8694 e^{-04}	-2.8431 e^{-04}	6.1910 e^{-04}	7.9966	7.9078	Passed
4.1.07	-0.0012	0.0091	-0.0012	7.9948	7.9055	Passed
4.1.08	-4.991 e^{-04}	0.0072	0.0017	7.9952	7.9062	Passed
4.2.01	-5.0900 e^{-04}	0.0101	8.3929 e^{-04}	7.9968	7.9066	Passed
4.2.02	-0.0019	0.0159	-0.0049	7.9954	7.9056	Passed
4.2.03	-0.0014	0.0059	0.0023	7.9972	7.9095	Passed
4.2.04	-1.3330 e^{-04}	0.0081	-0.0022	7.9966	7.9079	Passed
4.2.05	0.0013	0.0078	1.8927 e^{-04}	7.9955	7.9062	Passed
4.2.06	-7.9005 e^{-04}	-2.6753 e^{-04}	0.0030	7.997	7.9069	Passed
4.2.07	-0.0031	0.0034	-8.4341 e^{-04}	7.9969	7.9085	Passed

*Table **Error! No text of specified style in document.**.4 : Results of Correlation Coefficient and Shannon Entropy Analysis for SIPI Color Image Database*

Algorithm	Correlation Coefficients of Encrypted Image			Global Shannon entropy		
	Horizontal	Vertical	Diagonal	Red	Blue	Green
Proposed Algorithm	-0.0463	-4.1346e^{-04}	-9.9911e^{-04}	7.9968	7.9973	7.9971
Rehman et al [5] - 2018	0.0005	-0.0061	0.0010	7.9966	7.9972	7.9967
Liu et al [26] - 2018	0.0046	0.0043	-0.0006	-	-	-
Cai et al [27] - 2018	0.0046	-0.0028	0.0013	7.9992	7.9994	7.9993
Cai et al [28] - 2018	-0.0016	0.0013	5.666e^{-04}	7.9993	7.9994	7.9994
Kadir et al. [10] - 2017	0.0019	-0.0016	0.0019	7.9914	7.9915	7.9916
Niyat et al. [18] - 2017	0.0022	0.0001	-0.0017	7.9972	7.9973	7.9972
X.Wu et al.[29] - 2017	-0.0029	-0.0001	-0.0045	7.9903	7.9890	7.9893

*Table **Error! No text of specified style in document.**.5 : Comparison of the Average Correlation Coefficients and Global Shannon Entropy of Lena Image*

5.8.5. Key Sensitivity Analysis

A robust image cipher is more sensitive to keys [30]. A tiny change in key will provide a different cipher image. To prove key sensitivity, two different keys K1 and K2, are taken for encryption.

$$K1 = \begin{cases} x_0 = 0.25345233254129 \\ y_0 = 1.00054323461235 \\ z_0 = 0.25678915461231 \\ w_0 = 0.23564532314324 \end{cases}$$

$$K2 = \begin{cases} x_0 = 0.2534523325412\mathbf{1} \\ y_0 = 1.00054323461235 \\ z_0 = 0.2567891546123\mathbf{5} \\ w_0 = 0.23564532314324 \end{cases}$$

Figure 5.9(d) shows the difference between the two cipher images encrypted by K1 and K2. The difference shows that small changes in the keys will generate an entirely distinct cipher image, so the proposed cryptosystem is extremely sensitive to keys. NPCR and UACI are the other metrics that are used to evaluate key sensitivity [1], [31]. Table 5.4 shows the result of different test images encrypted using keys K1 and K2, and Table 5.5 shows that the proposed cipher has efficient security than some existing systems.

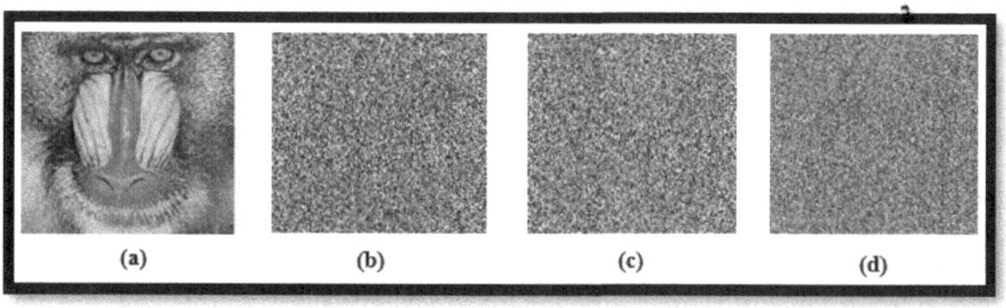

Figure 5.9 : Key sensitivity analysis (a) Original image (b) Ciphered image with original keys (c) Ciphered image with changed keys (d) Difference between (c) and (d)

Test Images	NPCR (%)			UACI (%)		
	Color Components			Color Components		
	Red	Green	Blue	Red	Green	Blue
Pepper	0.9962	0.9960	0.9960	0.3360	0.3357	0.3344
Baboon	0.9962	0.9960	0.9960	0.3346	0.3346	0.3352
Barbara	0.9962	0.9960	0.9960	0.3342	0.3347	0.3347
Boats	0.9962	0.9960	0.9960	0.3342	0.3347	0.3344
R, G, B Average	0.9962	0.9960	0.9960	0.3342	0.3354	0.3350

Table 5.4: NPCR and UACI Values of Different Test Images with Keys K1 and K2

Algorithm	Average of NPCR(R, G, B)	Average of UACI(R, G, B)
Proposed Algorithm	0.996215	0.334767
Wang et al. [30] - 2017	0.995823	0.332434
Sharif et al. [32] - 2017	0.995975	0.334438
Elgendy et al. [35] -2015	0.996073	0.333651
Xiangjun Wu et al. [19] - 2015	0.996000	0.334700

Table 5.5: Comparison of Key Sensitivity with One Bit Difference of Lena (4.2.04)

5.8.6. Quality Evaluation Metrics of Encrypted Image

The metrics taken for evaluating the quality of the encrypted image are (EQ), PSNR, and SSIM [33]. In Table 5.6, it can be identified that the average EQ for the encrypted image is greater than 230, which is large enough to resist. PSNR is another standard method used to measure the fidelity of an image by comparing the encrypted image with its corresponding original image. A lower PSNR value indicates that the cipher image is entirely different from the original image. Another metric employed to assess the quality of encryption is SSIM [34]. SSIM results fall within the range of (-1,1]. Lower values indicate that there is no similarity between the original and cipher image. Hence, a good cipher should have low PSNR and SSIM values and higher EQ values. Table 5.6 presents the EQ, PSNR, and SSIM results for different test images from the SIPI database, and Table 5.7 compares the EQ and PSNR results with those of existing systems. From the results in Tables 5.6 and 5.7, it transpires that the proposed cipher has a good encryption effect.

Test Image	EQ			PSNR			SSIM		
	Color Components			Color Components			Color Components		
	Red	Green	Blue	Red	Green	Blue	Red	Green	Blue
4.1.01	219	219	248	8.113	7.031	6.8090	0.008	0.006	0.005
4.1.02	250	232	286	6.622	6.083	6.0247	0.005	0.005	0.003
4.1.03	268	258	225	9.872	10.01	9.9811	0.011	0.011	0.011
4.1.04	242	.391	204	8.407	8.509	9.6675	0.009	0.009	0.010
4.1.05	291	3.285	192	9.769	8.761	8.2837	0.011	0.009	0.009
4.1.06	5.062	1.128	1.128	8.683	7.593	8.2781	0.006	0.008	0.010
4.1.07	289	242	201	8.463	7.998	9.4333	0.010	0.010	0.010
4.1.08	276	266	240	8.520	8.191	9.3321	0.011	0.009	0.008
4.2.01	228	6.992	212	7.556	7.244	8.1959	0.009	0.008	0.008
4.2.02	274	254	212	5.641	6.969	8.1959	0.009	0.010	0.010
4.2.03	250	244	286	8.932	9.506	8.5829	0.012	0.012	0.011
4.2.04	252	304	278	7.876	8.596	9.6274	0.009	0.009	0.010
4.2.05	248	219	215	8.198	7.872	7.9824	0.009	0.007	0.010
4.2.06	242	192	215	9.560	7.608	7.5755	0.010	0.011	0.009
4.2.07	289	2.331	15625	9.143	7.642	7.6804	0.009	0.009	0.007

Table 5.6: Results of EQ, PSNR and SSIM for Different Test Images

Algorithm	Lena			Baboon		
PSNR:	Red	Green	Blue	Red	Blue	Green
Proposed scheme	7.87	8.60	9.63	8.93	9.51	8.58
Rehman et al. [5] - 2018	7.87	8.57	9.67	8.93	9.50	8.56
Kalpana et al. [35] - 2015	10.37	10.59	11.92	11.37	11.72	11.99
Encryption Quality (EQ)						
Proposed scheme	252	304	278	250	244	286
Rehman et al. [5] - 2018	204	148	261	154	199	141

Table ***Error! No text of specified style in document.****.6 : Comparison of PSNR and EQ with existing systems*

5.8.7. Robustness Against Cipher Image Attack Analysis

Even sensitive images are transferred securely using some cryptosystem. Sometimes, cipher images are attacked during transmission through cropping and noise attacks. Hence, the corresponding receiver cannot obtain the original image even after decrypting the cipher image using the correct keys. A good encryption algorithm should resist cipher image attacks. Therefore, the reliability of the proposed cipher is tested by applying cropping and noise attacks.

5.8.7.1. Cropping Attack Analysis

The robustness of the proposed image cryptosystem against data loss during transmission is analyzed using crop attack analysis [18]. The encrypted Lena image is cropped at different densities, and the corresponding decrypted images are shown in Figure 5.10. In Figure 5.10(a-d), the encrypted image is cropped at ratios of 1/16, 1/8, 1/4, and 1/2, with the corresponding decrypted images shown in Figure 5.10(e-h). The main intent of this analysis is to determine whether the decrypted image of the cropped cipher image can be visually recognized. From Figure 5.10, it is evident that the proposed method works effectively even with 50% data loss. Thus, the proposed image cryptosystem is robust against cropping attacks.

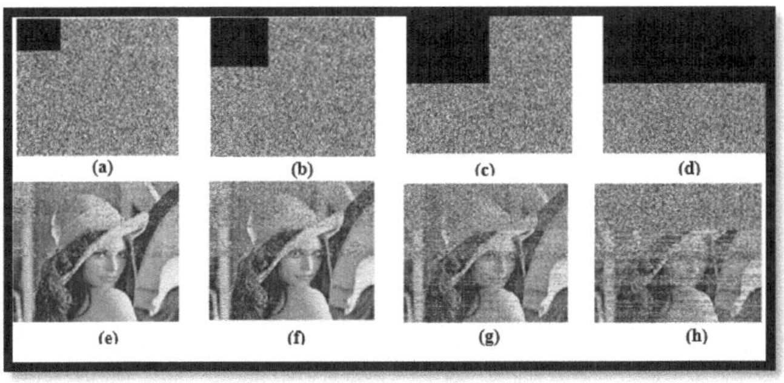

Figure 5.10 : Analysis of Cropping Attack : Encrypted Lena Cropped By The Ratio of (A) 1/16 (B) 1/8 (C) 1/4 (D) 1/2 . (E-H) Corresponding Decrypted Images of (A-D)

5.8.7.2. Noise Attack Analysis

Noise attack analysis is highly imperative to ensure the quality of the deciphered image after transmission over any channel [36]. In this context, salt and pepper noise (uniform distribution) and Gaussian noise (normal distribution) are intentionally added to the cipher images for testing. Salt and pepper noise is uniformly distributed. Due to this property, a high intensity of noise affects only a minimal number of pixels. The whole image is affected at an intensity of 0.5. Figure 5.11 (b1, b2, and b3) shows that the proposed cipher can withstand salt and pepper noise attacks up to an intensity of 0.2. Filter processing is required to de-noise the cipher image when it is affected by an intensity higher than 0.2, as given in Table 5.8. Gaussian noise is normally distributed, affecting each pixel. Due to this, even a small amount of Gaussian noise can highly degrade the original image. Figure 5.11 (c1–c4) illustrates the decryption results of images affected by different intensities. Figure 5.11 shows that even when the cipher image is affected by noise, the receiver can visualize the original image with some degradation after decrypting it.

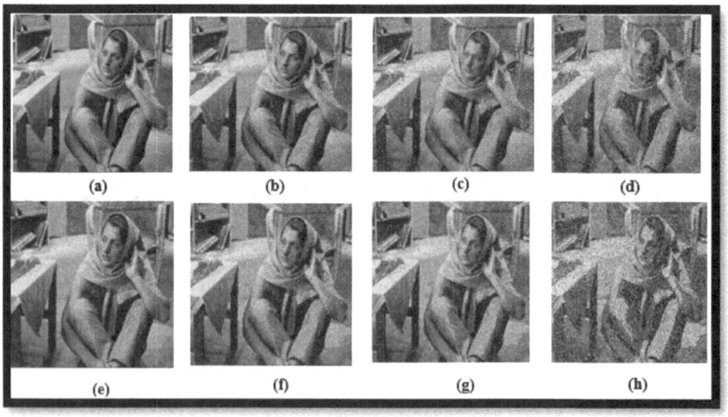

Figure ***Error! No text of specified style in document.****.10 : Noise attack analysis (a) Decrypted image not affected by noise (b, c and d) Decrypted cipher images affected by salt and pepper noise of intensities 0.01, 0.1 and 0.2; (e, f, g and h) Decrypted cipher images*

5.8.8. Measurement of Decryption Quality

The quality of the deciphered image is analyzed using objective and subjective methods. Objective methods such as PSNR and MSE are based on numerical comparison, while SSIM is the subjective method that provides better results than other quality metrics as it incorporates luminance, structure, and contrast information of the image to assess quality [37]. SSIM is calculated for images affected by crop attacks with different ranges and noise attacks with varying intensities, and the results are tabulated in Table 5.8. Both uniform and normal distribution noises are tested. Hence, the proposed method can withstand noise attacks.

Test Image	**Noisy and Crop Range**		**Decryption Quality**	
		SSIM value	**Similarity Range**	**Degradation Range**
Encrypted Barbara	Without noise and crop	1	100 %	0 %
Crop Range:				
Figure 5.10(d)	15 %	0.9122	91%	9%
Figure 5.10(e)	25 %	0.7311	73 %	27%
Figure 5.10(f)	50 %	0.4717	47 %	53%
Salt and pepper noise :				
Figure 5.11(b1)	0.01	0.8770	88 %	12 %
Figure 5.11(b2)	0.1	0.4592	46 %	54 %
Figure 5.11(b3)	0.2	0.2833	28 %	72 %
Gaussian noise :				
Figure 5.11(c1)	0.0001	0.7174	72 %	28 %
Figure 5.11(c2)	0.0005	0.5632	56 %	44 %
Figure 5.11(c3)	0.001	0.4950	50 %	50 %
Figure 5.11(c4)	0.01	0.2839	28 %	72 %

Table ***Error! No text of specified style in document.****.7 : Estimation of Decryption Quality Based on SSIM Results*

5.9. Computational Complexity Analysis

The overall computational complexity for the image size (M × N) is calculated using the number of iterations it takes to generate the chaotic key series and for the confusion and diffusion processes. Four chaotic series are generated. All four series with the size M or N is used for the confusion process and (M × N)/4 is used for the diffusion process. Number of pixels scrambled in confusion process is M × N for each component (R, G, and B). So the total number of iteration requests for the confusion process is 3(M × N). For the diffusion process, each pixel is computed for all three components. Hence, the total number of computations is 3(M × N). As a result, the total algorithm computational complexity is M or N + 25/4(M × N). After the constant notations are omitted, the total complexity becomes O (M × N) as M or N is smaller than (M × N).

5.10. Time Complexity Analysis

Efficient execution time is one of the significant parts of good cryptosystem. The environment used for implementation in Matlab16a with Intel(R) Core(TM) i7-6700 CPU @ 3.4 GHz and 16.0 GB RAM on Windows 8.1 OS. To evaluate, a standard Lena image is taken with different size (■(256 ×256,&512×512)). The average proposed method execution time of color and greyscale images are listed and compared in Table 5.9 and Table 5.10. The time comparison analysis proves that the proposed scheme has an efficient execution time. Encryption throughput (ETP) is also one of the important factors to evaluate the performance of the cryptosystem. Calculation for identifying ETP in megabyte per second (MBps) is given in Equation. (5.13).

$$ETP = \frac{Input\ image_{Size}\ (in\ Bytes)}{Encryption_{Time}\ (in\ Seconds)} \quad (5.13)$$

Image Size	Proposed Method	Luo et al. - 2018 [26]	Cai et al. - 2018 [27]	Huang et al. - 2018 [28]	Wu et al. - 2017 [23]
256 x 256 Execution time (Seconds)	1.186s	4.212s	1.1347s	1.0896s	3.6175s
ETP - (MBps)	0.474MBps	0.134MBps	0.496MBps	0.516MBps	0.1555MBps
512 x 512 Execution time (Seconds)	4.463s	8.308s	4.6058s	4.4113s	14.8119s
ETP - (MBps)	0.168MBps	0.090MBps	0.163MBps	0.170MBps	0.051MBps

*Table **Error! No text of specified style in document.**.8 : Comparison of Color Image Encryption*

Image Size	Proposed Method	Luo et al. - 2018 [26]	Cai et al. - 2018 [27]	Diab et al. - 2018 [28]	Xu et al. - 2016 [28]
256 x 256 Execution Time (Seconds)	0.431s	1.318s	0.4389s	1.2432s	3.1342s
ETP - (MBps)	0.145MBps	0.047MBps	0.1424MBps	0.050MBps	0.020MBps
512 x 512 Execution Time (Seconds)	1.186s	2.256s	1.8112s	4.8593s	12.6917s
ETP - (MBps)	0.211MBps	0.111MBps	0.138MBps	0.051MBps	0.020MBps

Table 5.10: Comparison of Greyscale Image Encryption

5.11. Chapter Summary

A novel method has developed for converting decimal value chaotic series to applicable integer form in the diffusion process. The proposed cryptosystem follows the architecture of confusion and diffusion. Before encryption, the proposed hexadecimal pre-processing is executed on chaotic series generated by the Lorenz system. In confusion, intra - pixels are scrambled by using the index value of the sorted pair of chaotic series. In diffusion, each pixel is represented in binary form, and binary merging and circular shifting operations are executed depend on keys, finally, XOR operation is executed between each layer pixels to obtain cipher image. The randomness of the chaotic series is assured by the Lorenz hyper chaotic map. Security and performance analysis proves that the proposed image cipher is strong enough to withstand different attacks. Consequently, the proposed scheme is very appropriate for secure image transmission and storage in real time applications.

5.12. References

i. Zheng, Y., & Jin, J. (2015). A novel image encryption scheme based on Hénon map and compound spatiotemporal chaos. *Multimedia Tools and Applications*, 74(18), 7803–7820.

ii. Fan, H., Li, M., Liu, D., & An, K. (2018). Cryptanalysis of a plaintext-related chaotic RGB image encryption scheme using total plain image characteristics. *Multimedia Tools and Applications*, 77(15), 20103–20127.

iii. Norouzi, B., & Mirzakuchaki, S. (2017). Breaking a novel image encryption scheme based on an improper fractional order chaotic system. *Multimedia Tools and Applications*, 76(2), 1817–1826.

iv. Tan, C. H., Prabowo, T. F., & Le, D. (2016). Breaking an ID-based encryption based on discrete logarithm and factorization problems. *Information Processing Letters*, 116(2), 116–119.

v. ur Rehman, A., Liao, X., Ashraf, R., Ullah, S., & Wang, H. (2018). A color image encryption technique using exclusive-OR with DNA complementary rules based on chaos theory and SHA-2. *Optik (Stuttgart)*, 159, 348–367.

vi. Chai, X., Fu, X., Gan, Z., Lu, Y., & Chen, Y. (2019). A color image cryptosystem based on dynamic DNA encryption and chaos. *Signal Processing*, 155, 44–62.

vii. Liu, W., Sun, K., & He, S. (2017). SF-SIMM high-dimensional hyperchaotic map and its performance analysis. *Nonlinear Dynamics, 89*(4), 2521–2532.

viii. Chai, X., Yang, K., & Gan, Z. (2016). A new chaos-based image encryption algorithm with dynamic key selection mechanisms. *Multimedia Tools and Applications*, 1–21.

ix. Wu, P. (n.d.). Research on digital image watermark encryption based on hyperchaos. *Watermark Encryption Based Pianhui Wu Doctor of Philosophy*, University of Derby.

x. Kadir, A., Aili, M., & Sattar, M. (2017). Optik color image encryption scheme using coupled hyper chaotic system with multiple impulse injections. *Optics - International Journal of Light and Electron Optics, 129*, 231–238.

xi. Ye, G., & Huang, X. (2016). A secure image encryption algorithm based on chaotic maps and SHA-3. *Security and Communication Networks, 9*, 2015–2023.

xii. Li, Y., Wang, C., & Chen, H. (2017). A hyper-chaos-based image encryption algorithm using pixel-level permutation and bit-level permutation. *Optics and Lasers in Engineering, 90*, 238–246.

xiii. Mirzaei, O., Yaghoobi, M., & Irani, H. (2012). A new image encryption method: Parallel sub-image encryption with hyper chaos. *Nonlinear Dynamics, 67*(1), 557–566.

xiv. Yuan, H. M., Liu, Y., Lin, T., Hu, T., & Gong, L. H. (2017). A new parallel image cryptosystem based on 5D hyper-chaotic system. *Signal Processing: Image Communication, 52*, 87–96.

xv. Wang, X., & Zhang, H. (2015). A novel image encryption algorithm based on genetic recombination and hyper-chaotic systems. *Nonlinear Dynamics, 1*(Online), 333–346.

xvi. Zhang, Q., Guo, L., & Wei, X. (2013). A novel image fusion encryption algorithm based on DNA sequence operation and hyper-chaotic system. *Optik (Stuttgart), 124*(18), 3596–3600.

xvii. Elgendy, F., Sarhan, A. M., Eltobely, T. E., El-Zoghdy, S. F., El-sayed, H. S., & Faragallah, O. S. (2015). Chaos-based model for encryption and decryption of digital images. *Multimedia Tools and Applications*, 1–25.

xviii. Yaghouti Niyat, A., Moattar, M. H., & Torshiz, M. N. (2017). Color image encryption based on hybrid hyper-chaotic system and cellular automata. *Optics and Lasers in Engineering, 90*(October), 225–237.

xix. Wu, X., Li, Y., & Kurths, J. (2015). A new color image encryption scheme using CML and a fractional-order chaotic system. 1–28.

xx. Eom, S., & Huh, J.-H. (2018). The opening capability for security against privacy infringements in the smart grid environment. *Mathematics, 6*(10), 202.

xxi. Eom, S., & Huh, J. H. (2018). Group signature with restrictive linkability: Minimizing privacy exposure in ubiquitous environment. *Journal of Ambient Intelligence and Humanized Computing,* 0(0), 1–11.

xxii. SIPI Image Database - Misc. (n.d.).

xxiii. Wu, X., Zhu, B., Hu, Y., & Ran, Y. (2017). A novel color image encryption scheme using rectangular transform-enhanced chaotic tent maps. *IEEE Access,* 5, 6429–6436.

xxiv. Xu, L., Li, Z., Li, J., & Hua, W. (2016). A novel bit-level image encryption algorithm based on chaotic maps. *Optics and Lasers in Engineering, 78,* 17–25.

xxv. Wu, Y., Zhou, Y., Saveriades, G., Agaian, S., & Noonan, J. P. (2013). Local Shannon entropy measure with statistical tests for image randomness. *Information Sciences (New York), 222,* 323–342.

xxvi. Luo, Y., Zhou, R., Liu, J., Qiu, S., & Cao, Y. (2018). An efficient and self-adapting colour-image encryption algorithm based on chaos and interactions among multiple layers. *Multimedia Tools and Applications,* 77(20), 26191–26217.

xxvii. Cai, S., Huang, L., Chen, X., & Xiong, X. (2018). A symmetric plaintext-related color image encryption system based on bit permutation. *Entropy, 20*(4), 1–20.

xxviii. Huang, L., Cai, S., Xiao, M., & Xiong, X. (2018). A simple chaotic map-based image encryption system using both plaintext related permutation and diffusion. *Entropy, 20*(7), 1–20.

xxix. Wu, X., Wang, K., Wang, X., & Kan, H. (2017). Lossless chaotic color image cryptosystem based on DNA encryption and entropy. *Nonlinear Dynamics, 90*(2), 855–875.

xxx. Diab, H. (2018). An efficient chaotic image cryptosystem based on simultaneous permutation and diffusion operations. *IEEE Access, 6,* 42227–42244.

xxxi. Miao Zhang, X. T. (2015). A new algorithm of the combination of image compression and encryption technology based on spatiotemporal cross chaotic map. *Multimedia Tools and Applications, 74,* 11255–11279.

xxxii. Mollaeefar, M., Sharif, A., & Nazari, M. (2017). A novel encryption scheme for colored image based on high level chaotic maps. *Multimedia Tools and Applications, 76*(1), 607–629.

xxxiii. Norouzi, B., Mirzakuchaki, S., Seyedzadeh, S. M., & Mosavi, M. R. (2014). A simple, sensitive and secure image encryption algorithm based on hyper-chaotic system with only one round diffusion process. *Multimedia Tools and Applications, 71*(3), 1469–1497.

xxxiv. Naeem, E. A., Abd, M. M., El-sayed, H. S., Abd, F. E., & Faragallah, O. S. (2016). Wavelet fusion for encrypting images with a few details. *Computers and Electrical Engineering, 54,* 450–470.

xxxv. Kalpana, J., & Murali, P. (2015). An improved color image encryption based on multiple DNA sequence operations with DNA synthetic image and chaos. *Optics and Laser Engineering, 126*(24), 5703–5709.

xxxvi. Yao, L., Yuan, C., Qiang, J., Feng, S., & Nie, S. (2017). Asymmetric color image encryption based on singular value decomposition. *Optics and Lasers in Engineering, 89*, 80–87.

xxxvii. Kumar, M., & Vaish, A. (2017). Encryption of color images using MSVD in DCST domain. *Optics and Lasers in Engineering, 88*, 51–59

CHAPTER 6

Lightweight Bio-crypt Architecture to Secure Biometric Templates on IoT Applications

6.1. Introduction

The next generation of digital communication is the Internet of Things (IoT), which interconnects and establishes communication between various electronic devices such as actuators, sensors, smart devices, etc. The main goal of IoT is to make these devices available to all connected on the Internet [1]. Information can be sent and received by these devices over a network using their respective Internet Protocol (IP) addresses. Numerous IoT applications have been invented and provide services to different sectors like healthcare, military, government, education, security, surveillance, and banking systems, making our lives more convenient. Depending on the sector, IoT devices must produce and manage massive data. Conventional computing and storage platforms might not be able to handle the huge volume of data delivered by IoT devices. Many researchers have evidenced that cloud computing is a suitable platform for managing large-scale data because the cloud environment allows developers to access and store massive amounts of data remotely without delay [2].

Nevertheless, while IoT has enhanced the quality of our lives, IoT security remains a significant concern in today's world because many IoT applications are vulnerable to different attacks, putting human lives in danger. Five common types of attacks that occur in the IoT environment

[3] are Botnet, Man-In-The-Middle Attack (MIMA), Information and Individual Identity Theft, Social Engineering, and Denial-of-Service (DoS) attacks. These attacks endanger human lives because IoT applications are integrated into daily activities. Hence, security problems have become a key concern in the IoT environment, potentially hindering the development of IoT applications or causing significant data loss. Hewlett Packard reports that 70% of common IoT devices are vulnerable to attacks [4]. These vulnerabilities are caused by the absence of encrypted transmission, inadequate authentication and authorization, insufficient website security configurability, and poor physical security.

Identity-based authentication is one feasible solution to ensure the security of devices in IoT. The primary goal of authentication is to preserve confidentiality and privacy while ensuring the security of IoT devices and infrastructure. There are three major categories of IoT authentication: knowledge-based, ownership-based, and biometric-based identity verification. Knowledge-based and ownership-based identity authentication are traditional IoT security methods that use passwords, PINs, OTPs, and objects like smart cards as key attributes for authentication [5]. Numerous authentication protocols based on these two categories have been developed by researchers. However, it has been proven that these methods are insufficient for trustworthy identity assurance because these attributes can be easily stolen or misplaced [6]. IoT security based on biometric authentication utilizes a person's physiological and behavioral characteristics as attributes, making them less susceptible to theft or misplacement. Commonly used physiological attributes include fingerprints, face recognition, palm scans, iris scans, hand veins, and DNA. Gait, signature, and voice are common human behavioral attributes used for biometric authentication [7].

6.2. Benefits of Biometric Authentication for IoT Applications

Nowadays, most IoT applications recommend employing biometric-based authentication for security. Figure 6.1 defines different IoT application systems that require biometric security. In a smart home, every electronic device and smart door lock system can be controlled by smart devices. For these smart devices, biometric authentication provides a high level of security. By using an IoT healthcare system, a doctor can authorize themselves using biometric traits to access patient reports stored in a database. Currently, IoT-based smart farming has become very popular in agriculture for monitoring crop fields with the help of sensor devices, which are activated by the concerned owners trusted through biometric security. The benefits of a smart IoT transport system include vehicle-to-vehicle communication, public transport management, and traffic monitoring. For instance, a traffic police officer can identify the owner of a car using biometric verification. In connection with these scenarios, it can be concluded that the biometric system plays a vital role in IoT security. This makes the researchers to develop different types of biometric security protocol for IoT, some of the protocols are discussed as follows.

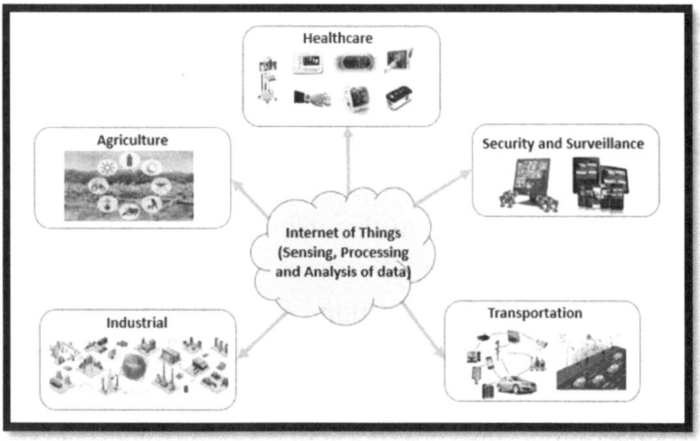

Figure ***Error! No text of specified style in document.****.11 : Framework of Iot Environment in Various Applications*

Biometric security can be implemented using different attributes, such as gait, palm print, fingerprints, face, and speech. These attributes are human-dependent and more reliable compared to traditional (knowledge- and token-based) approaches, as they are unique to each individual, greatly reducing the possibility of identity theft [8]. However, the EU General Data Protection Regulation 2016/679 suggests that each individual's biometric identity should be protected under privacy protection rights [9]. Leakage of biometric identity should be prevented by securing biometric templates. The main objective of this study is to provide dual-layer security for biometric templates transmitted over wireless channels using low-power consumption encryption methodologies.

6.3. State of the Art

Traditional encryption systems like MD5, RC5, DES, and AES are not suitable for protecting images due to their large pixel capacity and the high correlation among pixels. Meanwhile, chaotic properties have attracted many researchers, leading to the development of numerous chaotic map-based image encryption architectures for secure image transmission. Some chaos-based biometric template security protocols are discussed below.

Han et al. [10] developed a novel fingerprint encryption approach based on chaotic series generated by multi-scroll chaotic attractors. The initial value acts as a private key, and the diffusion process is executed using the XOR operation between the discrete chaotic series and the biometric image.

Bhatnagar et al. [11] proposed a biometric security application using a dual-tree wavelet transform. A Markov map is used to randomize the biometric template, and the image is further confused using the Hilbert space-filling curve to obtain an encrypted biometric template.

An enhanced biometric image transmission security framework was proposed by Bhatnagar et al. [12]. In this framework, biometric images are shuffled using the Fractional Wave Packet Transform (FrWPT) domain, with transform orders chosen randomly using a chaotic map. Further encryption is applied using an affine transform. The robustness and efficiency of the framework were demonstrated through various validation analyses on biometric images.

A novel technique [13] for double image encryption was developed using multiple hyper-chaotic maps. Chen and Rossler hyper-chaotic maps were employed for encrypting face biometric images. Furthermore, the developed algorithm's efficiency and security were demonstrated against multiple attacks.

A multiple single- and high-dimensional chaotic map-based biometric template cryptosystem was proposed by Hsiao et al. [14]. The main strength of this cryptosystem is its large key space, making it resistant to attacks against biometric images. Furthermore, this cryptosystem passed the NIST suite, proving that biometric images are securely transmitted over the network.

Loukhaoukha et al. [15] proposed an efficient and secure fingerprint cryptosystem utilizing wavelet domain permutation and a substitution process. The Rubik's cube technique is applied in the permutation process to randomly shuffle pixel positions, enhancing security. The robustness and efficiency of this approach were demonstrated through differential and statistical attack results.

A novel two-dimensional fusional chaotic map-triggered biometric cryptosystem was proposed by employing a diffusion-confusion architecture [16]. The index value of the fusional chaotic map is used for permutation, and the XOR operation is applied between the confused image and the chaotic series to achieve diffusion. Further attack analyses on the encrypted template demonstrated the cryptosystem's robustness and efficiency.

In recent years, DNA biomolecule-triggered image cryptosystems have fascinated various cryptography research groups due to their inherent features, such as parallel processing and high-speed data computation with lower energy consumption. Different research groups have enhanced image cryptosystems by integrating DNA computing with chaos.

Chai et al. [17] proposed an image cryptosystem combining a two-dimensional logistic map with DNA computing. Additionally, a plain image-dependent DNA encoding and decoding process was implemented to provide resistance against chosen and known plaintext attacks. Chai et al. [18] further developed a fusion of the two-dimensional Logistic Adjacent Sine (LAS) map and a new one-dimensional chaotic map. The chaotic series generated by the LAS map was used for confusion, while the series from the latter map was used to determine DNA encoding rules. DNA XOR arithmetic was employed for diffusion. Seed keys were generated using SHA-256 with a plain image to enhance plain image sensitivity, resulting in an efficient cryptosystem.

Liu et al. [19] developed a new spatial chaos mechanism for DNA encoding and employed a logistic system's chaotic series to generate the DNA key image. DNA XOR was then applied between the scrambled DNA image and the key image to produce the encrypted image.

Zhang et al. [20] introduced a new quantum chaotic map that is more sensitive to initial seed keys than existing chaotic maps. This heightened sensitivity increases the cryptosystem's complexity, with the chaotic series dynamically selecting rules for DNA encoding, while DNA addition logic is used for encryption.

All the image ciphers discussed above rely on chaos and DNA computing, which share common structures for DNA encoding:

The pixels of an image are first converted into an 8-bit binary form. The bits are then divided into sets of two-tuples, yielding the possibilities {00, 01, 10, 11}. These are mapped to their corresponding DNA codes {A, T, C, G}.

According to the complementary rule, A pairs with T, while C pairs with G, allowing only eight types of DNA encoding.

In all types of DNA cryptosystems, DNA XOR or addition and subtraction operations are executed for the diffusion process. However, DNA-triggered image cryptosystems do not run on DNA computers for high-speed execution; rather, DNA computation methods are applied to binary value logical operations.

If DNA-based image cryptosystems are not designed properly, they can be vulnerable to passive attacks. The cryptosystem in [21] was cryptanalyzed in [22] using only five sets of chosen original-cipher images. Additionally, the cryptosystem in [23] was compromised by various cryptanalysts[24]–[26] using only 4PQ/3+14PQ/3+14PQ/3+1 pairs of original and cipher images, where P and Q represent the dimensions of the images. DNA-based image cryptosystems in [27], [28] were also cryptanalyzed in [29], [30] using chosen-plaintext attacks.

Considering the advantages and disadvantages of DNA-based image cryptosystems, along with the need for dual-layer security for biometric images, this study proposes a new methodology for DNA encoding and encryption. By integrating a two-dimensional Logistic Sine Map, we develop a biometric image cryptosystem with increased complexity and efficiency. The following section discusses the fundamentals of the proposed biometric cryptosystem.

6.4. Two Dimensional Logistic - Sine Map (2D LSM)

In [16], a new fusional 2D-LSM chaotic map is proposed by combining 2D Logistic map and 1D sine map. Equation (6.1) represents the mathematic form of 2D LSM.

$$x_{i+1} = mod\left(\beta_1 \sin(x_i) + \left(\gamma_1(y_i^2)\right), 1\right)$$
$$y_{i+1} = mod(\beta_2 \sin(y_i) + \left(\gamma_2(x_i^2 + x_i y_i)\right), 1) \quad (6.1)$$

$2.75 \leq \beta_1, \beta_2 \leq 3.45, 0.15 \leq \gamma_1 \gamma_2 \leq 0.21 \; and \; 0 \leq X_0, Y_0 \leq 1$

The key values taken for this cryptosystem are initialized as follows.

$$\beta_1 = 3.1234987656754 \quad \beta_2 = 2.87654567253423$$
$$\gamma_1 = 0.5345437683457 \quad \gamma_2 = 0.34576898760987$$
$$X_0 = 0.876543456323 \quad Y_0 = 0.56789432345687$$

Randomness and non-periodicity of 2D LSM are demonstrated in [16]. From the demonstration, it can be identified the 2D LSM has more random behaviour than standard 2D Logistic map. Therefore, this chaotic map is employed for the current biometric cryptosystem. The chaotic series generated by the chaotic function is always in decimal form, so to convert into acceptable integer form, the hexadecimal based chaotic key series generation is taken from chapter 5. A brief description of chaotic key generation is discussed below.

Step 1: Generate $[size = (M \times N)/8]$ number of chaotic series using 2D LSM as given in Equation (6.2). Where M and N indicate the size of the biometric image (BIM).

$$LX = [\, lx_1, lx_2, lx_3 \dots \dots lx_{size}]$$
$$LY = [\, ly_1, ly_2, ly_3 \dots \dots ly_{size}] \quad (6.2)$$

Step 2: Generated chaotic series are converted into corresponding hexadecimal value using Equation (6.3)

$$[\, HX, HY\,] = num2hex[\, LX, LY\,] \quad (6.3)$$

Step 3: The final integer form chaotic series can be obtained by applying the fragmentation and modulo operation to each hexadecimal value of HX and HY as expressed in Equation. (6.4)

$$\begin{aligned} IX &= mod(Fragment(HX), 256) \\ IY &= mod(Fragment(HY), 256) \end{aligned} \quad (6.4)$$

IX and IY will be integer format chaotic series that will be used for executing XOR operation between image and key in diffusion phase.

6.5. DNA Encoding and Enciphering

A combination of four nucleotides (Adenine (A), Cytosine (C), Thymine (T), and Guanine (G)) forms the DNA sequence. In accordance with the complementary rule, T and C, as well as A and G, are complementary to each other, similar to how 11 and 10 are the complements of 00 and 01 in a digital environment. Subsequently, this common criterion makes it possible to convert any binary representation into DNA code form. As a consequence, any image can be converted into a DNA code. At first, each pixel of the image is converted into binary form and then translated into the corresponding DNA code, depending on the complementary rule given in Table 6.1.

As an illustration, if the intensity of the pixel value is [155], then its 8-bit binary form will be [00110111]. After this, the 8-bit binary value is fragmented into four 2-bit pairs like [00 11 01 11]. Finally, the 2-bit binary code is converted into a DNA sequence using the rule. For instance, if rule 6 is chosen, then the corresponding DNA sequence will be [A T A G]. After DNA encoding, DNA encryption is applied using one of the arithmetic operations, such as XOR, addition, or subtraction, as given in Table 6.2 and Table 6.3.

	1	2	3	4	5	6	7	8
A	00	00	01	01	10	10	11	11
T	11	11	10	10	01	01	00	00

G	01	10	00	11	00	11	01	10
C	10	01	11	00	11	00	10	01

*Table **Error! No text of specified style in document.**.9: DNA Encoding Rules*

+	A	G	C	T
A	A	G	C	T
G	G	C	T	A
C	C	T	A	G
T	T	A	G	C

Table 6.2: DNA Addition Table

XOR	A	G	C	T
A	A	G	C	T
G	G	A	T	C
C	C	T	A	G
T	T	C	G	A

*Table **Error! No text of specified style in document.**.10 : DNA XOR Table*

Most of the existing DNA image cryptosystems use complementary rules and arithmetic operations for encoding and encryption [31], [32]. The main pitfalls of these methodologies are that they require higher execution time and power consumption. To overcome this, a novel technique for DNA encoding and encryption is proposed in this work. In this technique, instead of fragmenting the binary pixels into four pairs, binary pixels are fragmented into pairs of four bits. For example, [00110111] is converted into [0011 0111], and then DNA encoding is applied using Table 6.4. The DNA encoding mapping table differs for each complementary rule. Table 6.4 is framed based on Rule 2, so for the binary [0011 0111], the corresponding DNA sequence will be [AT CT].

The computational complexity of DNA encoding for an image of size M×N in the existing technique is [M×N×4], whereas the proposed method requires only [M×N×2]. This makes the cryptosystem more efficient than the existing one. In addition, a novel DNA encryption method is proposed. Instead of using arithmetic or logical operations, a new DNA reverse-complement technique is employed for encryption, which requires less time than XOR and addition operations. Hence, the DNA sequence [AT CT] is first reversed, resulting in [TC TA], and then the complement is applied, yielding [AG AT].

Further, the complemented DNA is decoded into binary form based on Rule 2, which was chosen for DNA encoding. As per Rule 2, the binary representation of [AG AT] is [0010 0011]. To obtain the corresponding pixel value, the binary value needs to be converted into integer form, and finally, encrypted pixel values are obtained to achieve the encrypted biometric template.

The demonstration of the proposed DNA encoding and DNA encryption is shown in Figure 6.2. The computational complexity of DNA conversion for an image of size (M × N) in the old method is (M × N × 4), while in the proposed methodology, it is (M × N × 2). For encryption, a new DNA reverse-complement process is employed. The comparison of execution time and computational complexity between the old and new methodologies is given in Table 6.5. From the comparison, it can be identified that the proposed encoding and substitution process has better performance than the existing one.

Binary - Nucleotides	Binary - Nucleotides	Binary - Nucleotides	Binary - Nucleotides
0000 - AA	0100 - CA	1000 - GA	1100 - TA
0001 - AC	0101 - CC	1001 - GC	1101 - TC
0010 - AG	0110 - CG	1010 - GG	1110 - TG
0011 - AT	0111 - CT	1011 - GT	1111 - TT

Table 6.4: DNA Encoding Mapping Table for Rule 2

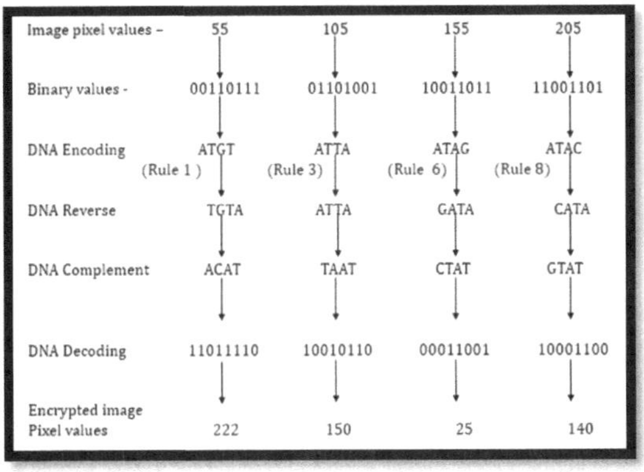

Figure 6.2: Demonstration of Proposed DNA Encoding and DNA Encryption

Algorithm	DNA Encoding	DNA encryption	Complexity of DNA encoding
Existing Scheme	4.51s	29.67s	(M × N × 4)
Proposed scheme	2.77s	1.13s	(M × N × 2)

Table ***Error! No text of specified style in document.****.11 : Comparison of DNA Encoding,*
DNA Encryption for 256 x 256 image

6.6. Proposed Biometric Cryptosystem

<u>6.6.1. Encryption</u>

The outline of the proposed biometric crypt architecture is demonstrated in Figure. 6.3. Confusion, DNA encoding, and encryption phases are discussed in the following sections.

6.6.2. Confusion of Odd Image and Even Image

The given input image is separated into two sub images based on odd column and even column. Each sub images are confused individually using the index of sorted chaotic series. Step by step procedure of confusion is discussed below.

Step 1: Separate the input biometric image BIM into ODD image and EVEN image by using the following Equation (6.5).

$$ODDimage_{p,q} = BIM_{i,j} \; if(mod(j,2) == 0) \; i,j,p = 1,2,\ldots\ldots M,N$$
$$ODDimage_{p,q} = BIM_{i,j} \; if(mod(j,2)! = 0) \; q = 1,2,\ldots\ldots N/2 \quad (6.5)$$

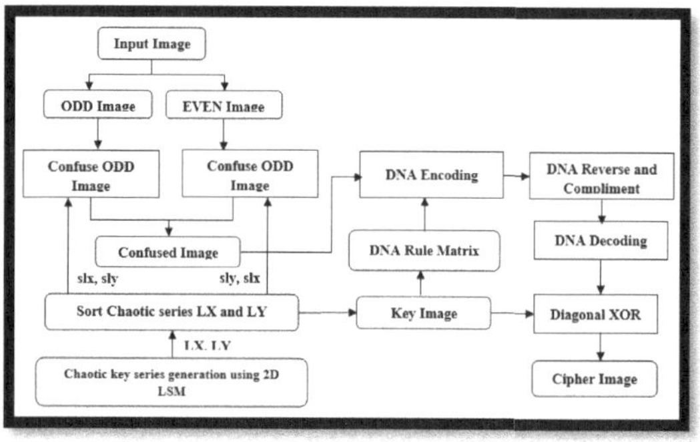

*Figure **Error! No text of specified style in document.**.12 : Outline of the Biomolecular and Chaos Based Biometric Cryptosystem*

Step 2: Sort the 2D-LSM chaotic series LX and LY to obtain the index of sorted chaotic series as given in Equation (6.6).

$[alx, slx] = sort(LX)\,; [aly, sly] = sort(LY)$ (6.6)

Now slx and sly are the index value of new sorted chaotic sequence LX and LY

Step 3: LX and LY chaotic series used to confuse ODD image and EVEN image. The mathematical representation of confusion is illustrated in Equation (6.7).

$$\begin{matrix} ODDimage_{p,q} \leftrightarrow ODDimage_{slx(i),sly(j)} \\ EVENimage_{p,q} \leftrightarrow EVENimage_{sly(i),slx(j)} \end{matrix} \quad where \quad \begin{matrix} p,i = 1,2,3,\dots\dots M \; or \; N \\ q,j = 1,2,3,\dots\dots N/2 \end{matrix}$$
(6.7)

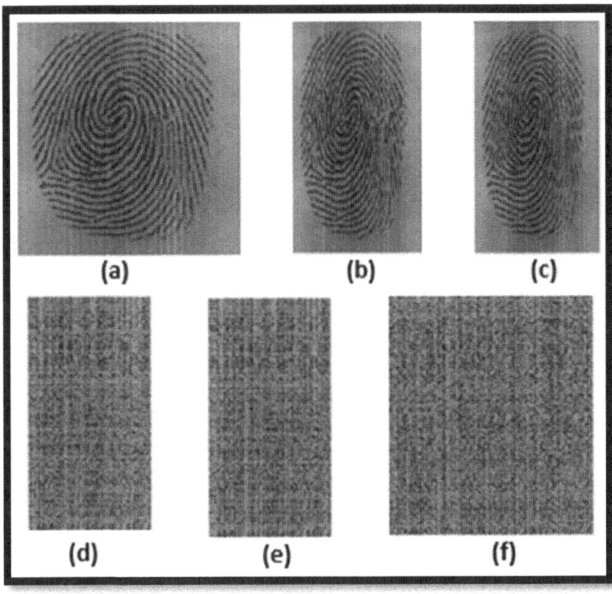

Figure 6.4: Result of Confusion Phase (A) Original Image (B, C) ODD And EVEN Image (D,E) Confused ODD And EVEN Image (F) Final Confused Image

Step 4: Combine the confused ODD image and EVEN image to get the final result of confusion as expressed in Equation (6.8)

$$\begin{matrix} CBIM_{i,j} = EVENimage_{p,q} \; if \; (mod\,(q,2) == 0) \\ CBIM_{i,j} = ODDimage_{p,q} \; if \; (mod\,(q,2) \,!= 0) \end{matrix} \quad where \quad \begin{matrix} i,j,p = 1,2,3 \dots\dots M \; or \; N \\ q = 1,2,3 \;\dots\dots N/2 \end{matrix}$$
(6.8)

CBIM represents Confused Biometric Image, which will be taken as an input for Diffusion process. The result of confusion process is demonstrated in Figure. 6.4.

6.6.3. Diffusion Phase: DNA Encoding and Enciphering

The diffusion phase is the combination of two phases: DNA encoding and DNA ciphering. In DNA encoding, the confused image is converted to the corresponding DNA code based on a rule that is selected randomly for each pixel. After that, DNA reverse and complement are applied to get the diffused image. First, the rule key for each pixel has to be created. This key is generated based on the combination of IX and IY, and the key matrix should be equal to the size of the input image. The following step-by-step procedure demonstrates the process of diffusion.

Step 1: Create the rule matrix using IX and IY. There are 8 DNA encoding rules, so the values stored in the rule matrix should be in the range between 0 and 7. First, the key image is created using IX and IY, and then that key image is converted into a rule matrix. The mathematical form of the creation of the key image and rule matrix is depicted in Equations (6.9 and 6.10).

$$keyimage_{i,j} = IX_k \; if(\, mod(j,2) == 0)$$
$$keyimage_{i,j} = IY_k \; if(\, mod(j,2) \,!= 0)$$
$$where \quad \begin{matrix} i,j = 1,2, \ldots \ldots M \; or \; N \\ k = 1,2, \ldots \ldots \left(\frac{M \times N}{2}\right) \end{matrix} \qquad (6.9)$$

$$DNARule_{i,j} = mod(keyimage_{(i,j)}, 8)$$
$$where \; i,j = 1,2,3 \ldots \ldots . M \; or \; N \qquad (6.10)$$

Step 2:

According to the rule matrix, each pixel in the confused image CBIM is converted into a DNA code, and then the reverse and complement operation is applied to each DNA code, as indicated in Equation (6.11). For further processing, the DNA code is decoded into the corresponding integer-form pixel value using the same DNA encoding rule and DNA Rule matrix.

$$DNABIM_{(i,j)} = DNA\_ENCODE(CBIM_{(i,j)}, DNARule_{(i,j)})$$
$$DNABIM'_{(i,j)} = DNA_{REVERSE\_COMPLIMENT}(DNABIM_{(i,j)}) \quad (6.11)$$
$$DBIM_{(i,j)} = DNA\_DECODE(CBIM_{(i,j)}, DNARule_{(i,j)})$$

Step 3:

Finally, the encrypted image is obtained by executing a diagonal XOR operation between the key image and the diffused image DBIM, as illustrated in the following Equation (6.12):

$$EBIM_{(i,j)} = bitxor(keyimage(_{N-1,N-1}), bitxor(DBIM_{(i+1j+1)}, keyimage_{(i-1,j-1)})$$
(6.12)

EBIM is the final Encrypted Biometric Image shown in Figure 6.5, which will be transferred securely on the network or stored in the Biometric database repository. Keys are securely shared by using key agreement and transmission protocols.

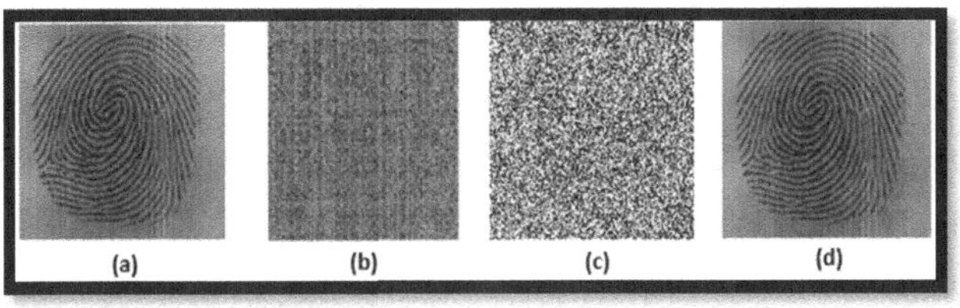

Figure 6.5: Experimental Result: (A) Original Image (B) Confused Image (C) Diffused Image (D) Decrypted Image

6.6.4. Decryption Phase

This phase is the reverse process of encryption, which has to be performed on the server side in a cloud environment. In the decryption phase, a chaotic series must first be generated using the same keys that were used for encryption. Then, the key image and DNA rule matrix are generated from the chaotic series. The received encrypted image is XORed diagonally with the key image and then translated into its corresponding DNA sequence. The DNA complement-reverse operation is applied to obtain the result of the reverse diffusion process. Further, the image undergoes reverse confusion to retrieve the original image. The illustration of the decryption phase is shown in Figure 6.5.

6.7. Experimental Results and Discussions

The proposed biometric cryptosystem is implemented using MATLAB 2016a. Sample fingerprint templates are selected from the repository DataBase3 (DB3) in the Fingerprint Verification Competition (FVC) 2002 [33], and palm print templates are selected from the Chinese Academy of Sciences' Institute of Automation (CASIA) image dataset [34]. The sample images used for simulation are (256×256) 8-bit grayscale images. The experimental results of different templates are shown in Figure 6.6.

The efficiency of the proposed biometric crypt is evaluated from two key perspectives. The first one is security analysis, which identifies the strength of the cryptosystem against numerical attacks. The second one is robustness analysis, which measures the performance of the cryptosystem against occlusion and noise attacks.

6.8. Security Analysis

6.8.1. Statistical Analysis

6.8.1.1. Histogram Analysis

As a result of confusion followed by the diffusion phase, the obtained final encrypted biometric image has highly uniform and randomized pixels, which do not reveal any meaningful information. A good cryptosystem should have the cipher image in the form of a uniform distribution of pixels [35].

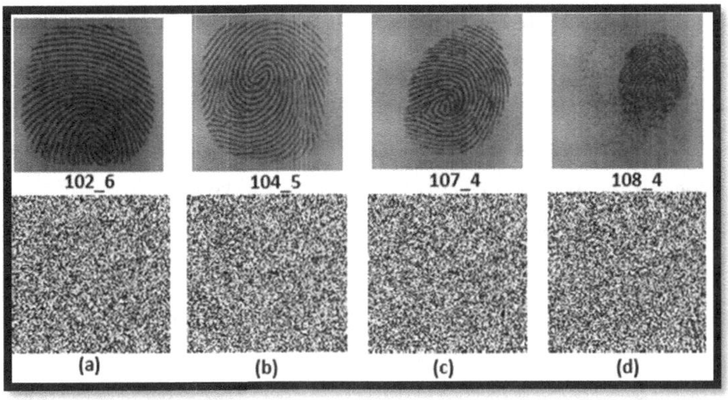

*Figure **Error! No text of specified style in document.**.13 : Experimental Results: First Row Shows the Original Fingerprint Images. Second Row Shows Its Corresponding Cipher Images*

Figure 6.7 shows the histogram of both the original and encrypted biometric template. From that, it can be realized that our proposed cryptosystem has achieved uniform and random distribution, which protects against any leakage of information related to the original template.

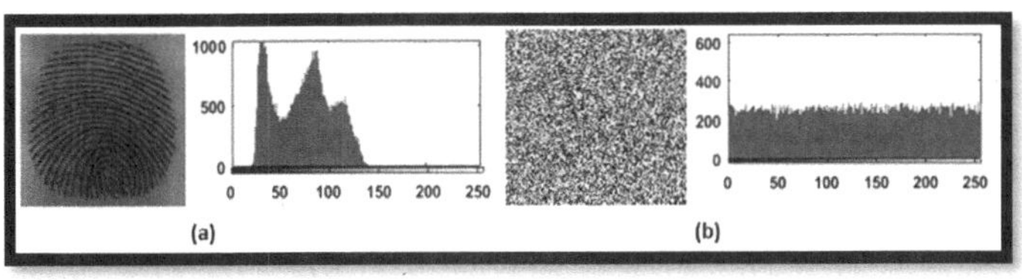

Figure 6.7: Histogram Analysis: (A) Original Fingerprint Histogram (B) Encrypted Template Histogram

6.8.1.2. Correlation Analysis

Most biometric template images have a high correlation among pixels because the same pixel values are displayed repeatedly in all directions of the image, such as horizontal, diagonal, and vertical. A good cryptosystem should break these correlations and create a cipher image with less correlation (nearest or less than 0) [36]. The diagrammatic representation of correlation among pixels in all three directions of the original and encrypted biometric templates is shown in Figure 6.8. The correlation numerical results of the cipher image in all directions are given in Table 6.6 and Table 6.7. From that, it has been accepted that the proposed cryptosystem greatly reduces the correlation among pixels to protect the image from numerical attacks, and the comparison results state that the proposed cryptosystem significantly reduces the correlation more than other cryptosystems.

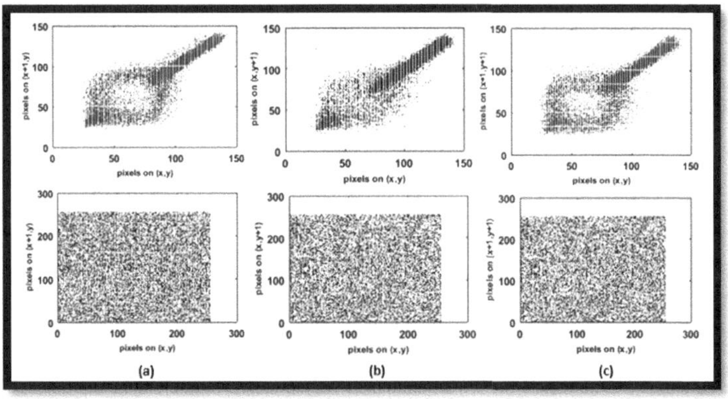

*Figure **Error! No text of specified style in document.**.14 : Correlation Analysis. Original and cipher image pixel correlation between pixels among (a) Horizontal Direction (HD) (b) Vertical Direction (VD)(c) Diagonal Direction(DD)*

6.8.1.3. Measure of Entropy

Entropy results state the level of uncertainty and random distribution of pixels in the cipher image. As stated by Shannon's theory, the approximate entropy value of an ideal image is 8. Hence, a good cryptosystem should have the entropy value of the cipher image equal to or nearest to 8 [37]. The entropy results of palm print test images and their comparison are in Table 6.7. From Table 6.7, it can be recognized that the proposed biometric cryptosystem has produced better random distribution than other systems.

Encrypted image of	Hsiao et al. [38] 2015			Rajendran et al. [16]			Proposed System		
	HD	VD	DD	HD	VD	DD	HD	VD	DD
102_6	0.0001	0.0001	0.0002	$-3.831e^{-4}$	-0.0042	0.0025	0.0024	-0.0118	-0.0090
104_5	0.0001	0.0003	0.0002	-0.0040	$-9.7e^{-04}$	0.0015	-7.30e-04	-0.0056	-0.0165
107_4	0.0002	0.0001	0.0002	-0.0068	$0.36e^{04}$	$-9.55e^{-04}$	0.0207	-0.0011	-0.0059
108_4	0.0002	0.0001	0.0002	-0.0056	$-1.3e^{-05}$	-0.0044	-0.0044	-00027	0.0093

Table 6.6: Comparison of Correlation Coefficient and Entropy Result of Fingerprint Template

Cipher image of	Horizontal direction	Vertical Direction	Diagonal direction	Entropy	Entropy result in [39]
003_l_460_02	-0.0169	-0.0049	-0.0139	7.9856	7.908847
001_l_460_01	-0.0017	0.0022	-0.0065	7.9881	7.939378
004_l_850_01	0.0013	-0.0127	-0.0049	7.9894	7.945920
003_l_460_01	0.0115	0.0089	-0.0030	7.9839	7.976059

Table 6.7: Comparison of Entropy and Correlation Result of Palmprint Template

6.8.2. Analysis of Key Sensitivity and Exhaustive Attacks

For any cryptosystem, length of the keys indicates the strength against brute force attack. Hence, the key size should be adequately large to fight against brute-force attacks. In the proposed crypt totally six keys are utilized, according to the IEEE floating standard [40], the floating precision range will have the maximum range of 10^{-14}. Thus the key size of the proposed crypt is 10^{84} which is sufficient to resist exhaustive attacks. Another essential requirement of cryptosystem is key sensitivity, even a small change in the key should highly affect the output of the cryptosystem [41]. To illustrate the sensitivity, two set of keys are selected with single digit variation. The first key key1 will be the same value as it is specified in section 1, for key2 the value of $[\gamma 1]$ changed to 0.534543768345. For simulation fifty pixels are selected from two fingerprint encrypted template (encrypted using key1 and key2) and those pixels are plotted in Figure 6.9. From figure 6.9 it will be able to identify that each encrypted biometric templates has different set of pixels. As a consequence, it can be identified that the proposed crypt has moral key sensitivity to withstand plaintext attack.

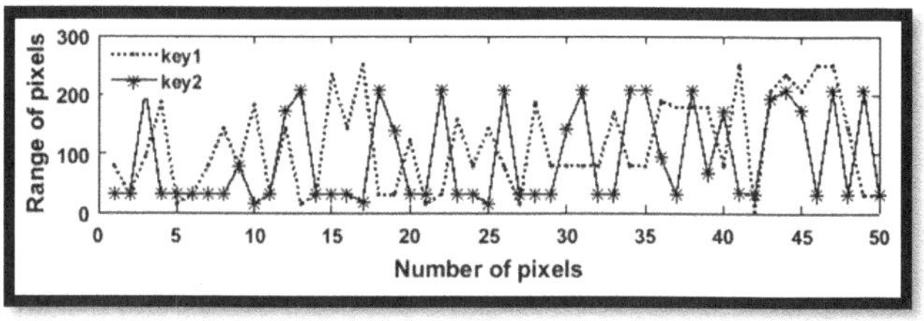

*Figure **Error! No text of specified style in document.**.15 : Key Sensitivity Analysis: Plot of Cipher Image Encrypted by Two Different Keys Key1 and Key2*

6.8.3. Robustness Analysis against Occlusion and Noise Attack

To analyze the security of the proposed biometric cryptosystem, its robustness against transmission attacks must be evaluated by applying occlusion and noise to the encrypted image [42]. For executing the occlusion attack, the encrypted template is intentionally cropped into three specific sizes ((50 × 50), (75 × 75), (125 × 125)), and it is decrypted using the correct key and procedure. The illustration of the cropped cipher template and their corresponding Decrypted Biometric Template (DBIM) are shown in Figure 6.10. Even though the original Biometric Template (BIM) is not 100% recovered after decryption, applying the median filter allows for the closest original template to be retrieved, and its quality is computed in the following section.

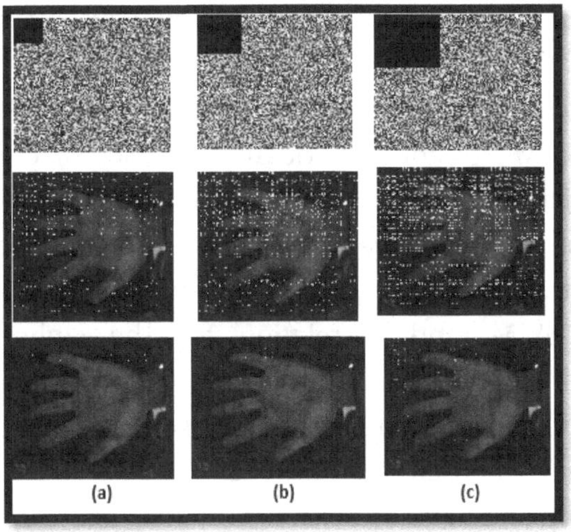

*Figure **Error! No text of specified style in document.**.16 : Robustness Analysis against Crop Attack: (First Row) Cipher Image Cropped by Specific Range (A) (50 X 50) (B) (75 X 75) (C) (125 X 125). (Second Row) Corresponding Decrypted Image. (Third Row) Decrypted Image After Applied the Median Filter*

Another attack that damages the cipher image during transmission is the noise attack. A good cryptosystem should maintain robustness even when the cipher image is attacked by different transmission attacks. To identify robustness against noise attacks, Gaussian noise and salt-and-pepper noise are intentionally applied to the cipher template, and the decrypted image is analyzed. The results are shown in Figure 6.11. The proposed system can withstand salt-and-pepper noise but cannot efficiently resist Gaussian noise. As a result even the encrypted template is affected by different noise, at the received end the original template can be visualized with some degradation.

6.8.4. Measurement of Decryption Quality

Two techniques are used to analyze the quality of the decrypted image: subjective and objective methods. PSNR and MSE fall under the objective method because these methods execute numerical comparisons to evaluate quality [43]. SSIM is another quality metric that falls under subjective methods and utilizes information on luminance, contrast, and structure of the image, providing better results than other methods [44]. The evaluated results of MSE, PSNR, SSIM, and correlation for the cipher templates affected by occlusion and noise attacks with different ratios are tabulated in Table 6.8. As a result, it can be concluded that the proposed biometric cryptosystem can withstand occlusion and noise attacks.

6.9. Computational Complexity

The complexity of the algorithm can be measured by identifying the number of loops and steps required to compute the confusion and diffusion phase. Here, two-dimensional grayscale images are utilized with height M and width N. Thus, the total number of pixels required for computation is (M × N). For chaotic key generation, ((M × N)/8) times the chaotic equation must be executed to generate the chaotic series, which will be used for the confusion and diffusion phase. In the confusion phase, the image is divided into ODD image and EVEN image, and then the confusion process is executed on each image separately with different keys. This requires (M × N) execution time. In diffusion, DNA encoding and enciphering require only (2 × M × N) execution time to convert the image to a DNA sequence and for applying Reverse and Complement. However, existing DNA encoding and ciphering techniques required (4 × M × N) execution time for executing the diffusion process. Thus, the proposed method significantly decreases execution time. Finally, an XOR operation is executed between the key image and DNA image, requiring (M × N) execution time. Hence, the overall computational complexity of the developed biometric cryptosystem is (6 × M × N), which is better compared to the state-of-the-art. Consequently, the proposed system has efficient computational time.

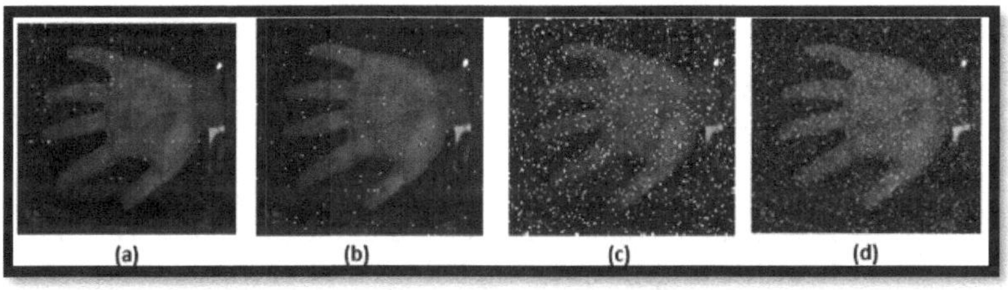

Figure ***Error! No text of specified style in document.****.17 : Noise Attack Analysis: Decrypted Image After Applied The Median Filter: Salt And Pepper Noise With Range (A) 0.001 (B) 0.01 (C) 0.1 (D) Gaussian Noise (Mean =0, Variance =0.0001)*

6.10. Chapter Summary

In this work, a novel DNA encoding and DNA reverse-complement method for encryption is proposed. The developed biometric cryptosystem provides dual-layer security for biometric images by combining the developed DNA computing method with a chaotic system. First, random key series are generated by computing the 2D Logistic Sine Map. Then, hexadecimal-based conversion of fractional chaotic keys to applicable integer form is executed. Second, in the confusion phase, images are divided into ODD and EVEN, and each one is confused separately using different chaotic key series. Afterward, the two confused images are merged to obtain the result of confusion. Finally, the confused image is subjected to DNA encoding and ciphering based on random keys. Results, security analysis, and comparative studies indicate that the proposed biometric cipher is more efficient and secure. Hence, this biometric cryptosystem is applicable for implementation in IoT client and server environments for securely transferring and storing biometric images used for authentication.

6.11. References

i. Hamidi, H. (2018). An approach to develop the smart health using Internet of Things and authentication based on biometric technology. *Future Generation Computer Systems, 86*, 306–316. https://doi.org/10.1016/j.future.2018.04.014

ii. Wazid, M., Das, A. K., Hussain, R., Succi, G., & Rodrigues, J. J. P. C. (2019). Authentication in cloud-driven IoT-based big data environment: Survey and outlook. *Journal of Systems Architecture, 97*, 185–196. https://doi.org/10.1016/j.sysarc.2019.04.009

iii. Obaidat, M. S., Rana, S. P., & Maitra, T. (2018). *Biometric security and Internet of Things (IoT) (Chapter 19)*. Elsevier.

iv. SecurityWeek. (n.d.). *70% of IoT devices vulnerable to cyberattacks, HP*. Retrieved from https://www.securityweek.com/70-iot-devices-vulnerable-cyberattacks-hp

v. El, H. A., & Hosni, M. M. (2019). Secure IoT communications for smart healthcare monitoring system. *International Journal of Computer Applications*, 1–14.

vi. Gupta, S., Buriro, A., & Crispo, B. (2019). DriverAuth: A risk-based multi-modal biometric-based driver authentication scheme for ride-sharing platforms. *Computers & Security, 83*, 122–139. https://doi.org/10.1016/j.cose.2019.03.002

vii. Jain, A. K., Nandakumar, K., & Nagar, A. (2008). Biometric template security. *EURASIP Journal on Advances in Signal Processing, 2008*, 1–17. https://doi.org/10.1155/2008/179713

viii. Punithavathi, P., & Geetha, S. (2019). Partial DCT-based cancelable biometric authentication with security and privacy preservation for IoT applications. *Journal of Electrical Engineering & Technology, 14*(6), 25487–25514. https://doi.org/10.1007/s42835-019-00094-w

ix. European Parliament. (2016). *EU regulation 2016/679*. Retrieved from http://ec.europa.eu/justice/data-protection/reform/index_en.htm

x. Han, F. (2007). Fingerprint images encryption via multi-scroll chaotic attractors. *Chaos, Solitons & Fractals, 35*(4), 931–939. https://doi.org/10.1016/j.chaos.2006.06.056

xi. Bhatnagar, G., Wu, J., & Raman, B. (2012). Fractional dual tree complex wavelet transform and its application to biometric security during communication and transmission. *Future Generation Computer Systems, 28*(1), 254–267. https://doi.org/10.1016/j.future.2011.04.004

xii. Bhatnagar, G., & Wu, Q. M. J. (2014). Enhancing the transmission security of biometric images using chaotic encryption. *Computer Standards & Interfaces, 36*(2), 203–214. https://doi.org/10.1016/j.csi.2013.08.005

xiii. Studies, A., & Playitas, Z. (2013). Double hyperchaotic encryption for security in biometric systems. *International Journal of Computer Applications, 13*(1), 55–68.

xiv. Hsiao, H., & Lee, J. (2015). Fingerprint image cryptography based on multiple chaotic systems. *Signal Processing, 113*, 169–181. https://doi.org/10.1016/j.sigpro.2014.09.015

xv. Loukhaoukha, K., Refaey, A., Zebbiche, K., & Shami, A. (2018). Efficient and secure cryptosystem for fingerprint images in wavelet domain. *Signal Processing, 143*, 9325–9339. https://doi.org/10.1016/j.sigpro.2018.07.031

xvi. Rajendran, S., & Doraipandian, M. (2018). Biometric template security triggered by two-dimensional logistic sine map. *Journal of Biometrics & Biostatistics, 9*(4), 1–10. https://doi.org/10.4172/2155-6180.1000312

xvii. Chai, X., Chen, Y., & Broyde, L. (2017). A novel chaos-based image encryption algorithm using DNA sequence operations. *Optics and Lasers in Engineering, 88*, 197–213. https://doi.org/10.1016/j.optlaseng.2016.11.016

xviii. Chai, X., Gan, Z., Yuan, K., Chen, Y., & Liu, X. (2019). A novel image encryption scheme based on DNA sequence operations and chaotic systems. *Optics and Lasers in Engineering, 115*, 219–237. https://doi.org/10.1016/j.optlaseng.2018.08.004

xix. Liu, P., Zhang, T., & Li, X. (2019). A new color image encryption algorithm based on DNA and spatial chaotic map. *Multimedia Tools and Applications, 78*(11), 14823–14835. https://doi.org/10.1007/s11042-019-08027-0

xx. Zhang, J., & Huo, D. (2018). Quantum image encryption algorithm based on chaotic system and DNA coding. *Journal of Southwest Jiaotong University, 53*(6), 1142–1149. https://doi.org/10.35741/issn.0258-2724.53.6.43

xxi. Zhang, Q., & Liu, L. (2013). DNA coding and chaos-based image encryption algorithm. *Journal of Computational and Theoretical Nanosciences, 10*(2), 341–346. https://doi.org/10.1166/jctn.2013.3113

xxii. Zhang, Y. (2016). Comments on "DNA coding and chaos-based image encryption algorithm." *Journal of Computational and Theoretical Nanosciences, 13*(7), 4025–4035. https://doi.org/10.1166/jctn.2016.5740

xxiii. Zhang, Q., Guo, L., & Wei, X. (2013). A novel image fusion encryption algorithm based on DNA sequence operation and hyper-chaotic system. *Optik, 124*(18), 3596–3600. https://doi.org/10.1016/j.ijleo.2013.01.036

xxiv. Xie, T., Liu, Y., & Tao, J. (2014). Breaking a novel image fusion encryption algorithm based on DNA sequence operation and hyper-chaotic system. *Optik, 125*, 7166–7169. https://doi.org/10.1016/j.ijleo.2013.07.081

xxv. Zhang, Y., Wen, W., & Su, M. (2014). Cryptanalyzing a novel image fusion encryption algorithm based on DNA sequence operation and hyper-chaotic system. *Optik, 125*, 1562–1564. https://doi.org/10.1016/j.ijleo.2013.10.021

xxvi. Zhang, Y. (2017). Cryptanalysis of a novel image fusion encryption algorithm based on DNA sequence operation and hyper-chaotic system. *Optik, 8*(2), 223–229. https://doi.org/10.1016/j.ijleo.2017.02.042

xxvii. Zhang, Q., & Wei, X. (2013). A novel couple images encryption algorithm based on DNA subsequence operation and chaotic system. *Optics, 124*(23), 6276–6281. https://doi.org/10.1016/j.ijleo.2013.07.019

xxviii. Zhen, P., Zhao, G., & Min, L. (2017). Chaos-based image encryption scheme combining DNA coding and entropy. *Multimedia Tools and Applications, 76*(12), 14021–14033. https://doi.org/10.1007/s11042-017-4460-9

xxix. Zeng, L., & Liu, R. (2015). Cryptanalyzing a novel couple images encryption algorithm based on DNA subsequence operation and chaotic system. *Optik, 126*(24), 5022–5025. https://doi.org/10.1016/j.ijleo.2015.08.045

xxx. Su, X., Li, W., & Hu, H. (2017). Cryptanalysis of a chaos-based image encryption scheme combining DNA coding and entropy. *Multimedia Tools and Applications, 76*(12), 14021–14033. https://doi.org/10.1007/s11042-017-4419-9

xxxi. Soni, R., Johar, A., & Soni, V. (2013). An encryption and decryption algorithm for image based on DNA. *Proceedings of the 2013 International Conference on Communication Systems and Networks Technology, CSNT 2013*, 478–481. https://doi.org/10.1109/CSNT.2013.116

xxxii. Zhang, Q., & Wei, X. (2013). A novel couple images encryption algorithm based on DNA subsequence operation and chaotic system. *Optik, 124*(23), 6276–6281. https://doi.org/10.1016/j.ijleo.2013.07.019

xxxiii. Biometrics Ideal Test. (2020). *Biometrics Ideal Test.* Retrieved from http://biometrics.idealtest.org

xxxiv. CASIA Palmprint Database. (n.d.). *CASIA Palmprint Database.* Retrieved from http://biometrics.idealtest.org/

xxxv. Wu, J., Liao, X., & Yang, B. (2017). Color image encryption based on chaotic systems and elliptic curve ElGamal scheme. *Signal Processing, 141*, 109–124. https://doi.org/10.1016/j.sigpro.2017.04.007

xxxvi. Chai, X., Fu, X., Gan, Z., Lu, Y., & Chen, Y. (2019). A color image cryptosystem based on dynamic DNA encryption and chaos. *Signal Processing, 155*, 44–62. https://doi.org/10.1016/j.sigpro.2018.10.004

xxxvii. Han, C. (2019). An image encryption algorithm based on modified logistic chaotic map. *Optik (Stuttgart), 181*, 779–785. https://doi.org/10.1016/j.ijleo.2018.12.089

xxxviii. Hsiao, H. I., & Lee, J. (2015). Fingerprint image cryptography based on multiple chaotic systems. *Signal Processing, 113*, 169–181. https://doi.org/10.1016/j.sigpro.2014.09.015

xxxix. Hikal, N. A., & Eid, M. M. (2018). A new approach for palmprint image encryption based on hybrid chaotic maps. *Signal Processing, 145*, 131–139. https://doi.org/10.1016/j.sigpro.2017.09.018

xl. Wu, J., Liao, X., & Yang, B. (2018). Image encryption using 2D Hénon-Sine map and DNA approach. *Signal Processing, 153*, 11–23. https://doi.org/10.1016/j.sigpro.2018.02.019

xli. Maddodi, G., Awad, A., Awad, D., Awad, M., & Lee, B. (2018). A new image encryption algorithm based on heterogeneous chaotic neural network generator and DNA encoding. *Multimedia Tools and Applications, 77*(15), 24701–24725. https://doi.org/10.1007/s11042-018-6224-5

xlii. Babaei, A., Motameni, H., & Enayatifar, R. (2020). A new permutation-diffusion-based image encryption technique using cellular automata and DNA sequence. *Optik (Stuttgart), 203*, 163–175. https://doi.org/10.1016/j.ijleo.2019.11.004

xliii. Li, C., Luo, G., & Li, C. (2018). A parallel image encryption algorithm based on chaotic Duffing oscillators. *Multimedia Tools and Applications, 77*(15), 19193–19208. https://doi.org/10.1007/s11042-018-6029-0

xliv. Karakiş, R., Güler, I., Çapraz, I., & Bilir, E. (2015). A novel fuzzy logic-based image steganography method to ensure medical data security. *Computational Biology and Medicine, 67*, 172–183. https://doi.org/10.1016/j.compbiomed.2015.02.012

CHAPTER 7
Conclusion

7.1. Conclusion

Three individual units — chaotic pseudo random generator, chaos and DNA-based image cryptosystems are developed as part of this integrated approach. To begin with, a fusional PRNG is developed to generate pseudo random numbers. This chaos-based PRNG is created by combining a 1D Chebyshev map and a 2D cross chaotic map. The developed 2D CCM achieves an enhanced key space of 1056 with improved chaotic behaviour and unpredictable random series. The key size of the developed 2D CCM is higher than 2128 and this is sufficient to withstand brute force attacks. Furthermore, the randomness of the chaotic sequence generated by 2D CCM is evaluated using the statistical NIST test suite. The chaotic key sequences successfully pass all the statistical test cases and produce a probability result value (P-Value > 0.01), thereby the generated chaotic sequence are truly random. The developed 2D CCM plays a vital role in the chaos based cryptosystem as it serves as a random key generator.

A fusional 2D CCM map based image cryptosystem is developed and implemented for accomplishing the confidentiality of greyscale medical images. The developed chaos based cryptosystem is employed SHA-256 to generate the seed key of 2D CCM based on plain images and used to accomplish the integrity of the cryptosystem. The confusion and the diffusion phases of the developed cryptosystem use the chaotic key sequence that is generated by the 2D CCM for encrypting the pixels of the medical images. In the diffusion process, a new dynamic bit-flipping technique is used to make the cryptosystem suitable for both 8-bit greyscale medical image and also 15-bit DICOM image. A comprehensive analyses are carried out to test the robustness and efficiency of the proposed cryptosystem. Experimental results show that the developed crypt architecture is highly sensitive to the chaotic key series of 2D CCM and has the ability to withstand brute force attacks with key spaces higher than 2310 (>2128). The developed model is efficient and has the strength to withstand statistical attacks by having the least correlation coefficient (approximately 0) and achieves the maximum entropy of 7.9976 for selected test images. Results of entropy, NPCR, and UACI achieve significant levels and proves that the cipher image has a random distribution of pixels and helps the developed cryptosystem resist differential attacks. Considering the results of security analysis and comparing them with state of the art, the proposed model proves to be more secure than the other medical image cryptosystems.

A part of this study devotes itself to improving the confidentiality of color images with hyper chaotic map. The key contribution of this study is to reduce the pre-processing time of hyper chaotic series to increase real time performance. In the proposed pre-processing technique, the required number of chaotic series to be generated is greatly reduced from the original image size to ¼ of the original image size. As a result, the proposed cryptosystem requires lesser computational time, memory space and works faster than the earlier techniques. In terms of security, a novel random bit-level merging and circular shifting process is employed in the diffusion process to increase the security level. Security and performance analysis of the cryptosystem proves the efficiency and robustness of the proposed model against statistical, differential, and exhaustive attacks. Additionally, the pre-processing unit greatly increases the throughput of the developed hex-chaos based color image crypt architecture from 0.1555 MBps to 0.474MBps over software implementation.

Finally, an integrated image cryptosystem is developed by integrating chaos with bio-molecular DNA computing to enhance the security of biometric images in IoT applications. A new model of DNA encoding and encryption is used to increase the real time performance by reducing computational time from 4.51s to 2.77s for DNA encoding and 29.67s to 1.13s for DNA encryption. This makes the cryptosystem easily implementable on smart devices. The proposed model is compared with state of the art models, and the comparative results prove that the developed methodology is more efficient than the others in terms of encryption level and robustness against various attacks.

7.2. Scope for Future Work

The present study highlights the design and development of multi-layered security algorithms to enhance the security of different types of images in various applications. This work has given rise to new ideas that can be used to improve the security of images as discussed in the below section:

7.2.1. Extending the use of Chaos for Securing Videos

Majority of videos are represented in three dimensions (3D). Videos are composed of series of frames, wherein each frame is treated as a separate image. This makes the cryptosystems developed for images applicable for encrypting videos. Video data is frequently transmitted in compressed form by adapting intra frame compression technique. The developed cryptosystems can be applied successfully on intra frames or on sensitive frames to ensure the security of videos during transmission and storage.

7.2.2. Incorporating Public Key with Chaos based Cryptosystems

All the image cryptosystems designed and developed in this study are symmetric key algorithms. Hence, they may suffer from problems related to key distribution. The only viable alternative is to adopt a public key infrastructure to create the seed key of the chaotic map. The developed cryptosystems can be extended by sharing the secret seed key via public key exchange protocols to provide a dual layer of security for multimedia content during transmission and storage.

Appendix A: List of Publications

The thesis is based on the following publications:

i. Rajendran, S., Krithivasan, K., Doraipandian, M., et al. (2020). Fast pre-processing hex chaos triggered color image cryptosystem. *Multimedia Tools and Applications,* 79(12), 12447–12469. https://doi.org/10.1007/s11042-019-08396-1

ii. Rajendran, S., Krithivasan, K., & Doraipandian, M. (2021). A novel cross cosine map based medical image cryptosystem using dynamic bit-level diffusion. *Multimedia Tools and Applications.* https://doi.org/10.1007/s11042-021-10798-z

iii. Rajendran, S., Manivannan, D., Manikandan, R., et al. (2021). Lightweight bio-chaos crypt to enhance the security of biometric images in Internet of Things applications. *Wireless Personal Communications.* https://doi.org/10.1007/s11277-021-08342-1

iv. Rajendran, S., Krithivasan, K., & Manivannan, D. (submitted). An image cipher based on bio-molecular hyper chaotic system with dual diffusion scheme. *Distributed and Parallel Databases.*

Publications: Scopus

i. Sujarani, R., & Manivannan, D. (2020). Chaos-based secure medical image transmission model for IoT-powered healthcare systems. *International Conference on Computational Research and Data Analytics (ICCRDA-2020) – IOP Conference Series.*

ii. Sujarani, R., & Manivannan, D. (2021). Design of medical image cryptosystem triggered by fusional chaotic map. In *Intelligent Data Communication Technologies and Internet of Things: Proceedings of ICICI 2020* (pp. 395-409). Springer Singapore.

iii. Sujarani, R., & Manivannan, D. (2019). Construction of two-dimensional cubic-tent-sine map for secure image transmission. *Communications in Computer and Information Science, ATIS 2019, 1116,* 51-61.

iv. Sujarani, R., Abilashaa, & Manivannan, D. (2019). Elliptic curve blended cross chaos-based secure image communication. *International Journal of Recent Technology and Engineering, 8*(3), 4481-4484.
v. Sujarani, R., & Manivannan, D. (2018). A nonlinear two-dimensional logistic-tent map for secure image communication. *International Journal of Information and Computer Security, 10*(2-3), 201-215.
vi. Sujarani, R., & Manivannan, D. (2018). Biometric template security triggered by two-dimensional logistic sine map. *Procedia Computer Science, 143*, 794-803.
vii. Sujarani, R., & Manivannan, D. (2018). A dual-layer chaos-triggered image cryptosystem. In *Proceedings of the 2nd International Conference on Communication and Electronics Systems, ICCES 2017* (pp. 224-229).
viii. Sujarani, R., & Manivannan, D. (2017). Chaotic map-based random image steganography using LSB technique. *International Journal of Network Security, 19*(4), 593-598.Sujarani, R., & Manivannan, D. (2017). A non-linear two-dimensional Henon-sine chaotic map based image cryptosystem. *International Journal of Pure and Applied Mathematics, 115*(7), 215-221.
ix. Sujarani, R., & Manivannan, D. (2017). A chaos-based double-layer secure data hiding in confused image. *International Journal of Pure and Applied Mathematics, 117*(16), 517-524.